CLEAN AIR

EARTH • AT • RISK

EARTH • AT • RISK

CLEAN AIR

by Edward Edelson

Introduction by
Russell E. Train

Chairman of
the Board of Directors,
World Wildlife Fund and
The Conservation Foundation

CHELSEA HOUSE PUBLISHERS

new york   philadelphia

CHELSEA HOUSE PUBLISHERS
EDITOR-IN-CHIEF: Remmel Nunn
MANAGING EDITOR: Karyn Gullen Browne
COPY CHIEF: Mark Rifkin
PICTURE EDITOR: Adrian G. Allen
ART DIRECTOR: Maria Epes
ASSISTANT ART DIRECTOR: Noreen Romano
MANUFACTURING DIRECTOR: Gerald Levine
SYSTEMS MANAGER: Lindsey Ottman
PRODUCTION MANAGER: Joseph Romano
PRODUCTION COORDINATOR: Marie Claire Cebrián

EARTH AT RISK
Senior Editor: Jake Goldberg

Staff for *Clean Air*
ASSOCIATE EDITOR: Karen Hammonds
COPY EDITOR: Christopher Duffy
EDITORIAL ASSISTANT: Danielle Janusz
PICTURE RESEARCHER: Nisa Rauschenberg
DESIGNER: Maria Epes
LAYOUT: Marjorie Zaum

3 5 7 9 8 6 4

Library of Congress Cataloging-in-Publication Data
Edelson, Edward.
   Clean air/Edward Edelson; introduction by Russell E. Train.
      p.   cm.—(Earth at risk)
   Includes bibliographical references and index.
   Summary: Discusses the devastating effects of population
growth and industry on air quality; the different types of
pollutants that can be found in the atmosphere; the health and
economical effects of pollution; and ways to clean up the air.
   ISBN 0-7910-1582-3
        0-7910-1607-2 (pbk.)
      1. Air—Pollution—Juvenile literature. 2. Air quality
management—Juvenile literature. [1. Air—Pollution. 2. Air
quality management. 3. Pollution. 4. Environmental protection.]
   I. Title. II. Series.   91-23252
   TD883.13.E34 1992   CIP
   363.73′92—dc20   AC

C O N T E N T S

INTRODUCTION

Russell E. Train
Administrator, Environmental Protection Agency, 1973 to
1977; Chairman of the Board of Directors, World Wildlife
Fund and The Conservation Foundation

There is a growing realization that human activities increasingly
are threatening the health of the natural systems that make life possible
on this planet. Humankind has the power to alter nature fundamentally,
perhaps irreversibly.

This stark reality was dramatized in January 1989 when *Time*
magazine named Earth the "Planet of the Year." In the same year, the
Exxon *Valdez* disaster sparked public concern over the effects of human
activity on vulnerable ecosystems when a thick blanket of crude oil
coated the shores and wildlife of Prince William Sound in Alaska. And,
no doubt, the 20th anniversary celebration of Earth Day in April 1990
renewed broad public interest in environmental issues still further. It is
no accident then that many people are calling the years between 1990
and 2000 the "Decade of the Environment."

And this is not merely a case of media hype, for the 1990s will
truly be a time when the people of the planet Earth learn the meaning of
the phrase "everything is connected to everything else" in the natural
and man-made systems that sustain our lives. This will be a period when
more people will understand that burning a tree in Amazonia adversely
affects the global atmosphere just as much as the exhaust from the cars
that fill our streets and expressways.

Central to our understanding of environmental issues is the
need to recognize the complexity of the problems we face and the

relationships between environmental and other needs in our society. Global warming provides an instructive example. Controlling emissions of carbon dioxide, the principal greenhouse gas, will involve efforts to reduce the use of fossil fuels to generate electricity. Such a reduction will include energy conservation and the promotion of alternative energy sources, such as nuclear and solar power.

The automobile contributes significantly to the problem. We have the choice of switching to more energy efficient autos and, in the longer run, of choosing alternative automotive power systems and relying more on mass transit. This will require different patterns of land use and development, patterns that are less transportation and energy intensive.

In agriculture, rice paddies and cattle are major sources of greenhouse gases. Recent experiments suggest that universally used nitrogen fertilizers may inhibit the ability of natural soil organisms to take up methane, thus contributing tremendously to the atmospheric loading of that gas—one of the major culprits in the global warming scenario.

As one explores the various parameters of today's pressing environmental challenges, it is possible to identify some areas where we have made some progress. We have taken important steps to control gross pollution over the past two decades. What I find particularly encouraging is the growing environmental consciousness and activism by today's youth. In many communities across the country, young people are working together to take their environmental awareness out of the classroom and apply it to everyday problems. Successful recycling and tree-planting projects have been launched as a result of these budding environmentalists who have committed themselves to a cleaner environment. Citizen action, activated by youthful enthusiasm, was largely responsible for the fast-food industry's switch from rainforest to domestic beef, for pledges from important companies in the tuna industry to use fishing techniques that would not harm dolphins, and for the recent announcement by the McDonald's Corporation to phase out polystyrene "clam shell" hamburger containers.

Despite these successes, much remains to be done if we are to make ours a truly healthy environment. Even a short list of persistent issues includes problems such as acid rain, ground-level ozone and smog, and airborne toxins; groundwater protection and nonpoint sources of pollution, such as runoff from farms and city streets; wetlands protection; hazardous waste dumps; and solid waste disposal, waste minimization, and recycling.

Similarly, there is an unfinished agenda in the natural resources area: effective implementation of newly adopted management plans for national forests; strengthening the wildlife refuge system; national park management, including addressing the growing pressure of development on lands surrounding the parks; implementation of the Endangered Species Act; wildlife trade problems, such as that involving elephant ivory; and ensuring adequate sustained funding for these efforts at all levels of government. All of these issues are before us today; most will continue in one form or another through the year 2000.

Each of these challenges to environmental quality and our health requires a response that recognizes the complex nature of the problem. Narrowly conceived solutions will not achieve lasting results. Often it seems that when we grab hold of one part of the environmental balloon, an unsightly and threatening bulge appears somewhere else.

The higher environmental issues arise on the national agenda, the more important it is that we are armed with the best possible knowledge of the economic costs of undertaking particular environmental programs and the costs associated with not undertaking them. Our society is not blessed with unlimited resources, and tough choices are going to have to be made. These should be informed choices.

All too often, environmental objectives are seen as at cross-purposes with other considerations vital to our society. Thus, environmental protection is often viewed as being in conflict with economic growth, with energy needs, with agricultural productions, and so on. The time has come when environmental considerations must be fully integrated into every nation's priorities.

One area that merits full legislative attention is energy efficiency. The United States is one of the least energy efficient of all the industrialized nations. Japan, for example, uses far less energy per unit of gross national product than the United States does. Of course, a country as large as the United States requires large amounts of energy for transportation. However, there is still a substantial amount of excess energy used, and this excess constitutes waste. More fuel efficient autos and home heating systems would save millions of barrels of oil, or their equivalent, each year. And air pollutants, including greenhouse gases, could be significantly reduced by increased efficiency in industry.

I suspect that the environmental problem that comes closest to home for most of us is the problem of what to do with trash. All over the world, communities are wrestling with the problem of waste disposal. Landfill sites are rapidly filling to capacity. No one wants a trash and garbage dump near home. As William Ruckelshaus, former EPA administrator and now in the waste management business, puts it, "Everyone wants you to pick up the garbage and no one wants you to put it down!"

At the present time, solid waste programs emphasize the regulation of disposal, setting standards for landfills, and so forth. In the decade ahead, we must shift our emphasis from regulating waste disposal to an overall reduction in its volume. We must look at the entire waste stream, including product design and packaging. We must avoid creating waste in the first place. To the greatest extent possible, we should then recycle any waste that is produced. I believe that, while most of us enjoy our comfortable way of life and have no desire to change things, we also know in our hearts that our "disposable society" has allowed us to become pretty soft.

Land use is another domestic issue that might well attract legislative attention by the year 2000. All across the United States, communities are grappling with the problem of growth. All too often, growth imposes high costs on the environment—the pollution of aquifers; the destruction of wetlands; the crowding of shorelines; the loss of wildlife habitat; and the loss of those special places, such as a historic structure or area, that give a community a sense of identity. It is worth noting that growth is not only the product of economic development but of population movement. By the year 2010, for example, experts predict that 75% of all Americans will live within 50 miles of a coast.

It is important to keep in mind that we are all made vulnerable by environmental problems that cross international borders. Of course, the most critical global conservation problems are the destruction of tropical forests and the consequent loss of their biological capital. Some scientists have calculated extinction rates as high as 11 species per hour. All agree that the loss of species has never been greater than at the present time; not even the disappearance of the dinosaurs can compare to today's rate of extinction.

In addition to species extinctions, the loss of tropical forests may represent as much as 20% of the total carbon dioxide loadings to the atmosphere. Clearly, any international approach to the problem of global warming must include major efforts to stop the destruction of forests and to manage those that remain on a renewable basis. Debt for nature swaps, which the World Wildlife Fund has pioneered in Costa Rica, Ecuador, Madagascar, and the Philippines, provide a useful mechanism for promoting such conservation objectives.

Global environmental issues inevitably will become the principal focus in international relations. But the single overriding issue facing the world community today is how to achieve a sustainable balance between growing human populations and the earth's natural systems. If you travel as frequently as I do in the developing countries of Latin America, Africa, and Asia, it is hard to escape the reality that expanding human populations are seriously weakening the earth's resource base. Rampant deforestation, eroding soils, spreading deserts, loss of biological diversity, the destruction of fisheries, and polluted and degraded urban environments threaten to spread environmental impoverishment, particularly in the tropics, where human population growth is greatest.

It is important to recognize that environmental degradation and human poverty are closely linked. Impoverished people desperate for land on which to grow crops or graze cattle are destroying forests and overgrazing even more marginal land. These people become trapped in a vicious downward spiral. They have little choice but to continue to overexploit the weakened resources available to them. Continued abuse of these lands only diminishes their productivity. Throughout the developing world, alarming amounts of land rendered useless by over-grazing and poor agricultural practices have become virtual wastelands, yet human numbers continue to multiply in these areas.

From Bangladesh to Haiti, we are confronted with an increasing number of ecological basket cases. In the Philippines, a traditional focus of U.S. interest, environmental devastation is widespread as deforestation, soil erosion, and the destruction of coral reefs and fisheries combine with the highest population growth rate in Southeast Asia.

Controlling human population growth is the key factor in the environmental equation. World population is expected to at least double to about 11 billion before leveling off. Most of this growth will occur in the poorest nations of the developing world. I would hope that the United States will once again become a strong advocate of international efforts to promote family planning. Bringing human populations into a sustainable balance with their natural resource base must be a vital objective of U.S. foreign policy.

Foreign economic assistance, the program of the Agency for International Development (AID), can become a potentially powerful tool for arresting environmental deterioration in developing countries. People who profess to care about global environmental problems— the loss of biological diversity, the destruction of tropical forests, the greenhouse effect, the impoverishment of the marine environment, and so on—should be strong supporters of foreign aid planning and the principles of sustainable development urged by the World Commission on Environment and Development, the "Brundtland Commission."

If sustainability is to be the underlying element of overseas assistance programs, so too must it be a guiding principle in people's practices at home. Too often we think of sustainable development only in terms of the resources of other countries. We have much that we can and should be doing to promote long-term sustainability in our own resource management. The conflict over our own rainforests, the old growth forests of the Pacific Northwest, illustrates this point.

The decade ahead will be a time of great activity on the environmental front, both globally and domestically. I sincerely believe we will be tested as we have been only in times of war and during the Great Depression. We must set goals for the year 2000 that will challenge both the American people and the world community.

Despite the complexities ahead, I remain an optimist. I am confident that if we collectively commit ourselves to a clean, healthy environment we can surpass the achievements of the 1980s and meet the serious challenges that face us in the coming decades. I hope that today's students will recognize their significant role in and responsibility for bringing about change and will rise to the occasion to improve the quality of our global environment.

Exhaust gases billow from a power plant smokestack. Fossil-fuel-burning power plants provide much of the electricity upon which the world now depends but are a major source of air pollution.

chapter 1

WHAT IS AIR POLLUTION?

The air in London, England, was thick and heavy in the early days of December 1952. A weather system had stalled over the British Isles, so cleansing winds did not blow away the sulfurous smoke that poured from the city's chimneys. Cars crawled along, their lights on at midday, as the sun shone dimly through a dark brown sky. This was more than the ordinary pea-soup fog for which the city was famous. As Londoners crowded into hospital emergency wards and doctors' offices, public health officials counted an appalling human toll: In less than a week, 3,500 to 4,000 deaths resulted from what newspapers often called the "black fog," a combination of fog and smoke containing harmful sulfuric acid and particles of soot.

Dirty air was nothing new to Londoners. As early as the 13th century, England's king Edward I banned the burning of *sea coles* while Parliament was in session. Smoke-laden air drew complaints in London and elsewhere in the world in the 19th century, and smoke-control legislation was passed in various cities, but such laws were not strictly enforced—pollution was essentially considered a minor nuisance, a small price to pay for industrial progress. The 1952 disaster in London, however, drove home the lesson that the thick fogs afflicting the city so regularly were really cases of severe, lung-damaging pollution, caused mostly by the combustion, or burning, of fossil fuels, primarily coal.

Events such as London's killer fog have sparked reforms. Indeed, London now has far fewer smoggy days thanks to clean air legislation. Many other heavily polluted cities and regions have passed laws to clean up their air as well. But the problem of air pollution remains—in fact, on a greater scale. Until recently, air pollution was essentially regarded as a local affair, not a widespread, global problem. Except in heavily polluted cities and industrial regions, clean air was generally not a major worry for most people. The situation has changed considerably. Virtually no

A double-decker bus inches its way through the severe smog that blanketed London, England, in December 1952.

area of the United States—indeed, of the world—is now free of concern about air pollutants.

Population growth, increased energy use, and the growing number of motor vehicles on the roads are among the leading factors that have made air pollution a large-scale, worldwide dilemma. Even in apparently pristine areas hundreds of miles from major sources of pollution, the effects of dirty air can be seen in lakes where fish populations have dwindled or disappeared, forests full of dying trees, and hazes that cloud once-clear vistas. The variety of pollutants in the earth's atmosphere has also increased, so the battle to clean the air requires attacks on many fronts. Growing awareness of the increasing damage caused by airborne pollutants has mobilized an international effort to seek solutions to this problem.

TYPES OF POLLUTANTS

The search for solutions starts with a definition of the problem: What pollutants foul the air and where do they come from?

Until recent decades, the term *air pollution* generally referred to London-type smog, a contraction of the words *smoke* and *fog*. This form of smog originates from the burning of low-grade coal containing a relatively high percentage of sulfur. Coal and other fossil fuels—for example, crude oil and natural gas—are combustible materials formed over eons from the partially decomposed remains of plants and animals.

When coal or oil is burned, carbon dioxide is released. Although not ordinarily considered an air pollutant, carbon dioxide is among the so-called greenhouse gases that trap heat in the earth's atmosphere and may be causing a global warming—a worldwide temperature increase. Sulfur and nitrogen oxide gases are also produced in fossil fuel combustion, along with particulates, or small particles, of ash, unburned fuel, or impurities from fuel. These emissions can be harmful by themselves; they can also react with oxygen, water vapor, and other compounds to produce new pollutants, including sulfuric and nitric acids and sulfate and nitrate compounds.

The acidic pollutants produced from sulfur and nitrogen oxide emissions fall to earth as *acid rain*. Acid rain is actually a misnomer for this phenomenon. Scientists use the term *acid deposition*, because acidic pollutants can fall in various forms of precipitation, including snow, fog, sleet, and dew, all called *wet deposition*, or they can combine with airborne particles to fall as *dry deposition*.

Coal-fired electric power plants are the largest source of sulfur dioxide emissions. Other major sources of this pollutant are factories, petroleum refineries, and metal smelters (where metal is separated from ore). At least 90% of sulfur dioxide emissions and more than 50% of nitrogen oxide emissions in the United States come from industrial and power plants. The largest single source of nitrogen oxides, however, is the motor vehicle.

The increased use of taller smokestacks by factories and power plants adds to the problem of acid rain and air pollution in general. These stacks release emissions higher into the atmosphere, causing them to remain aloft longer and to be transported great distances by winds.

When acidic substances settle to earth, they can upset the delicate chemical balance of nature. For example, fish and other inhabitants of lakes and rivers cannot tolerate too much acidity.

A sign along the Santa Monica Freeway in Los Angeles warns motorists of an impending smog. The California city's weather, geographic location, and traffic together cause frequent photochemical pollution there.

Trees also suffer from acid rain, which weakens them and makes them susceptible to disease. Around the globe, lakes have become sterile and forests are being damaged by acid fallout. Acids also leach toxic metals from soils and pipes, posing a potential health threat to people, and can corrode stone and masonry (brickwork), metals, rubber, and textiles.

In the years following World War II, a new type of air pollution emerged. It was most noticeable in the city of Los Angeles, California, where residents began to be troubled by days during which the sun shone brightly but the air became thick with an eye-stinging haze. All the standard methods for controlling London-style smog were tried in Los Angeles without success.

In the 1950s, scientists identified the Los Angeles problem as a different form of smog than that caused by coal combustion. They labeled the phenomenon *photochemical smog,* because it was caused by the action of sunlight upon certain polluting chemicals, which come mostly from the exhaust pipes of vehicles and, to a lesser extent, from fossil-fuel–burning industries. These pollutants include nitrogen oxides and various volatile organic compounds—mostly hydrocarbons, compounds of carbon and hydrogen that are the main constituents of gasoline.

Photochemical smog is caused primarily by incomplete or inefficient fuel combustion. When a car engine burns gasoline, some hydrocarbons pass through the engine unburned—when not enough oxygen is present—and some simply evaporate from the gas tank. Invisible, odorless yet poisonous carbon monoxide gas (CO) is also produced in incomplete combustion, when oxygen in the air combines incompletely with carbon in the fuel. (If sufficient oxygen is present, carbon combustion produces carbon dioxide [(CO_2)], and hydrocarbon combustion produces carbon dioxide and water.) Nitrogen oxides are created when high temperatures in an engine cause the oxygen and nitrogen in the air to combine chemically. This does not occur in nature because at ordinary temperatures nitrogen in air is chemically inert, or nonreactive. Hydrocarbons and nitrogen oxides react with oxygen in the presence of sunlight to produce a highly reactive substance called *ozone,* the main component of photochemical smog.

At ground level, ozone is a dangerous pollutant that can cause respiratory and other health problems. It also poses a serious threat to trees and crops by disrupting photosynthesis, the process by which plants derive energy using sunlight. It has been estimated that ozone pollution destroys $1 billion in farm crops in the United States annually. Ozone can also damage rubber and synthetic fabrics. To make matters worse, it is among the greenhouse gases believed to be causing a global warming.

The ground-level ozone found in smog should not be confused with ozone in the upper atmosphere. Although a damaging pollutant on earth, ozone in the stratosphere, a region of the atmosphere many miles above the earth, *protects* rather than harms people. Stratospheric ozone is created by the sun's ultraviolet radiation, which splits apart molecules of oxygen (O_2), producing oxygen atoms that then combine with other oxygen molecules to form ozone (O_3). Dangerous ultraviolet radiation is absorbed in the process and thus prevented from reaching the earth's surface, where it can harm people and other living things, causing such serious diseases as skin cancer.

There is much concern about depletion of the so-called ozone layer in the upper atmosphere, which has thinned in recent years because of synthetic chemicals—primarily chloro-fluorocarbons (CFCs)—that were developed for use as refrigerants, spray-can propellants, blowing agents for plastic-foam products such as fast-food containers, and for various other purposes. CFCs are harmless near the earth's surface. Eventually, however, they drift up to the stratosphere and release chlorine, a chemical that reacts with ozone, breaking it apart. International agreements have been reached to slow and eventually halt the production of ozone-destroying compounds, but it is uncertain whether these phaseouts will be sufficient to stop the ozone layer's destruction.

Industrial activity releases many other pollutants into the air. These include particulates of toxic elements such as cadmium, arsenic, chromium, mercury, and beryllium, whose sources include metal smelters, paper mills, and oil refineries; volatile organic compounds such as vinyl chloride and benzene, which come from plastics and chemical-manufacturing plants; radioactive substances such as iodine-131, uranium, and radon (discussed later in this chapter); and dioxin, a chemical released in various manufacturing processes and incineration that can cause a severe form of acne and other diseases.

In 1990, the Environmental Protection Agency (EPA) established limits for eight toxic substances: asbestos, mercury, vinyl chloride, arsenic, beryllium, benzene, sulfuric acid, and all radioactive substances. The agency also sponsors research to determine the hazards of a large number of other chemicals.

One toxic substance that is clearly a major health hazard is lead. This metal can accumulate in the body, slowly building to concentrations that can cause damage to many organs. Various products and industries emit lead, but the major source of atmospheric lead is gasoline. Fortunately, in the United States the amount of lead in gasoline has decreased steadily over the past two decades. This decrease came about when auto manufacturers began installing devices called *catalytic converters* in new cars to reduce exhaust emissions. Lead destroys the effectiveness of converters, so newer cars outfitted with these devices require unleaded gasoline.

INDOOR POLLUTION

A less well known but equally serious air pollution problem is occurring indoors. "Indoor pollutant levels are frequently higher than outdoors, particularly when buildings are tightly constructed to save energy," reported the EPA in 1990. The agency report noted that the most vulnerable people—the very old, the very young, and the ill—spend nearly all their time indoors. Office workers can also be affected by indoor pollutants, especially in modern buildings that have sealed windows and heavy insulation for better energy efficiency. Good ventilation requires a complete change of air two to four times an hour. In some energy-efficient buildings, an air change occurs less than once every eight hours, creating what has come to be known as the "sick building syndrome." A 1989 report by the EPA stated that indoor air pollution "may represent serious, acute and chronic health risks" and estimated that this type of pollution costs $1.2 billion annually in medical care as well as nearly $5 billion annually in lost work time.

Indoor pollutants include tobacco smoke; ozone, from such sources as electrostatic copying machines; formaldehyde, from building materials, furniture, and clothing; and asbestos, an insulating material formed from mineral fibers that is used in various building materials, heating pipes, electrical wiring, and even clothing. Crumbling asbestos can release fibers that easily become airborne; if inhaled or ingested they can cause severe lung diseases, including asbestosis, and cancer. Although the EPA prohibited most uses of this material in 1986, asbestos installed prior to the ban continues to pose a health hazard in many schools, offices, and other buildings.

Perhaps the most serious indoor pollutant is radon, a naturally occurring gas that is invisible and odorless. Radon gas results from the radioactive decay of a substance called radium, which is found in many kinds of rocks and soils. Radon seeps into houses through cracks or openings in their foundations. It can be inhaled into the lungs, where it releases damaging, cancer-

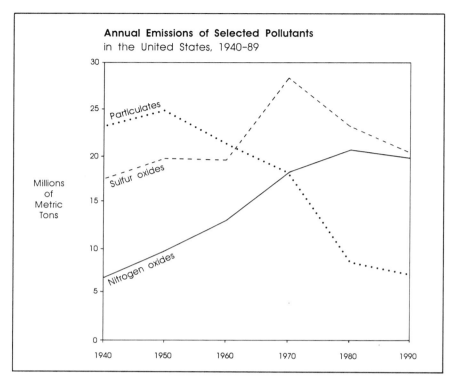

Annual Emissions of Selected Pollutants
in the United States, 1940–89

Millions of Metric Tons

Particulates

Sulfur oxides

Nitrogen oxides

Source: U.S. Environmental Protection Agency

causing radiation. Radon is blamed for 5,000 to 20,000 cases of lung cancer in the United States annually. Surveys by the EPA have determined that one house in five contains potentially harmful levels of this pollutant.

The dangers of radon were recognized in 1984, after a Pennsylvania nuclear plant worker named Stanley Watras kept setting off the radiation detector at the plant every night on his way home. It was not until Watras went through the detector in the morning, on his way in, that officials realized the problem was outside the plant. When they tested the Watras house, they found radon levels higher than those generally found in uranium mines. The house was made safe by sealing cracks and other entry points for radon and by improving ventilation, steps that are recommended for homes with a similar problem. Experts recommend that current and prospective homeowners have their houses tested for radon.

This litany of pollutants, indoors and out, may make it seem that no air is safe to breathe. In fact, air in the United States is safer in some respects than it was 20 or 30 years ago. Atmospheric concentrations of sulfur dioxide and lead, for example, have declined significantly. More reductions are needed, however. Although concentrations of nitrogen oxide and ozone in the air have leveled off in the United States, they remain at dangerously high levels in many cities on many days of the year. In 1988 the EPA estimated that at least 100 million Americans—more than 40% of the population—were exposed to unsafe levels of air pollution. Worldwide, 1 billion people— nearly one out of every five—are exposed to dangerous levels of pollutants, according to the World Health Organization. Growing numbers of cars and increasing electricity consumption threaten to create even worse air pollution in years to come.

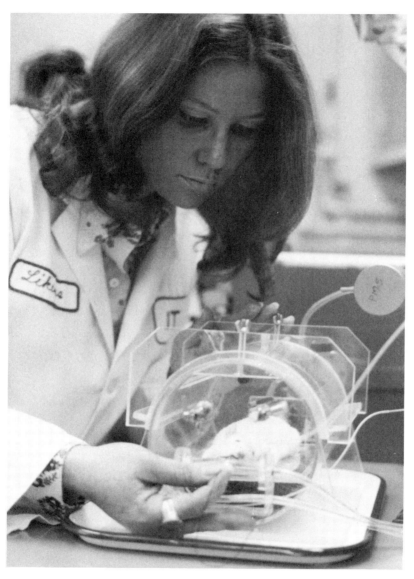

A technician monitors a laboratory rat at the Inhalation Toxicology
Research Institute in Albuquerque, New Mexico, where animals are
tested to determine the health effects of various air pollutants.

chapter 2

HEALTH EFFECTS OF AIR POLLUTANTS

A primary reason for wanting clean air is that polluted air can damage human health. Four catastrophes in recent history, in Europe and the United States, dramatically illustrate this potential. In each case, a period of severe pollution was accompanied by a sharp increase in illness and death, especially from respiratory diseases.

The first episode occurred in 1930 in Belgium's Meuse River valley, a major industrial region where the primary fuel was coal—a common thread in all four of these incidents. Atmospheric conditions during one week in December of that year caused what is known as a temperature *inversion*, in which a layer of warmer air overlaid a layer of cooler air, creating a sort of atmospheric lid over the valley that trapped coal combustion pollutants—sulfur oxides and particulates—in the air for an entire week. Sixty deaths were reported, and about 6,000 residents of the valley became ill with breathing problems and respiratory infections.

A similar incident occurred in 1948 in the industrial town of Donora, Pennsylvania, which also sits in a valley. This time a fog trapped pollutants above the town for several days, creating a brownish smog containing sulfur oxides and particulate-filled smoke belched from steel, zinc, and sulfuric acid factories. Twenty people died, and nearly 6,000 residents, or 40% of the population, suffered respiratory problems; the incidence was higher among persons already suffering from respiratory disease.

The toll was even greater in the infamous smog of December 1952 in London, when levels of both sulfur oxides and particulates rose far above normal, causing up to 4,000 deaths. The British Ministry of Health later concluded that "substances in the polluted fog caused irritation of the bronchi . . . and so accelerated death in those already suffering from diseases of the respiratory and cardiovascular system."

New York experienced several killer smogs in the 1960s. In one incident in November 1963, people who turned out for the annual Thanksgiving Day parade could see a brown pall hanging over the city. The air did not clear for several days. A later analysis attributed 58 deaths to the unusually severe pollution.

Air pollution in less dramatic, less visible forms threatens human health every day in many parts of the world. Its effects on people can be difficult to determine, however. Researchers who are trying to ascertain the overall health effects of polluted air face several challenges. They must determine how much injury results from different levels, or concentrations, of pollution; from varying lengths of exposure; and from different kinds of pollutants—for example, the damage caused by ozone versus sulfur oxides. They must also establish the effects of pollutants on persons of varying health and different ages. Three different methods of research, each with its strengths and weaknesses, are being used in efforts to answer these questions.

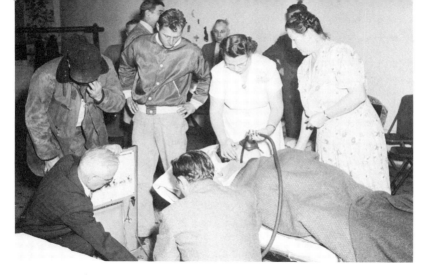

Oxygen is administered to one of the many Donora, Pennsylvania, residents who succumbed to a heavy smog in that industrial town in 1948.

One research technique involves exposing laboratory animals—usually mice or rats—to fixed levels of a pollutant for varied amounts of time. Animal experiments can be carefully controlled to single out specific effects of a pollutant on different aspects of health. Mice are not people, however; a correlation can be made between the results of experiments on other animals and the probable effects on humans, but not a perfect, one-to-one correspondence.

A second method uses humans as the experimental subjects. Researchers expose volunteers to fixed amounts of a pollutant in a controlled setting and measure the pollutant's effects on the lungs and other bodily parts. Human studies have limitations, however, because, among other things, volunteers cannot be exposed to levels of pollution that could cause serious damage. Extra precautions must be taken if the human guinea pigs are in the most vulnerable group—people with diseases of the lungs or heart.

In practice, both animal and human laboratory studies have another limitation: They generally involve only one pollutant, to achieve scientific accuracy. In the real world, people are usually not exposed to just one pollutant at a time. Even in Los Angeles and other cities where photochemical smog is the overwhelming problem, the mixture of pollutants in the air is not constant.

Epidemiological studies try to avoid the pitfalls of the previous two methods by looking at the health of large numbers of people exposed to everyday pollution levels in a community for long periods of time. One difficulty in these studies is determining levels of individual exposure to pollutants. Most epidemiological studies rely on monitoring stations to determine pollution levels. There are generally only a few such stations in any city, however, and these might not adequately measure the exposure of someone living miles away.

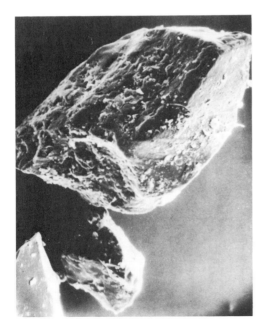

A common airborne particulate is coke dust, pictured here magnified more than 1,000 times. (Coke is a solid fuel produced from heated coal.)

In addition, personal habits affect exposure to polluted air. It is difficult to compare a person who spends most of the day watching television with one whose job requires outside work all day, someone who is indolent with someone who exercises vigorously, or a smoker with a nonsmoker. Nonetheless, scientists now have a reasonably good picture of the damaging effects of air pollution. In spite of all the confounding factors, it is clear that polluted air does damage health, and specific kinds of injury have been identified.

Ozone formed in photochemical smog has been linked to a number of health problems, although the effects of this pollutant are not completely understood. In laboratory studies using rats, ozone exposure has been shown to cause lung damage. With long-term exposure, the damage gets worse and can be triggered by lower concentrations of ozone. The animal also becomes more vulnerable to infection, indicating that ozone can damage the immune system.

Volunteers who are exposed to high levels of ozone experience chest pains and persistent coughing. Their lung capacity also declines, so they cannot breathe as well. These problems occur sooner if exercise is undertaken. The ozone levels that cause these problems in experiments are comparable to those commonly found in the polluted air over Los Angeles. Ozone also appears to aggravate chronic respiratory problems such as asthma, bronchitis, and emphysema, lung conditions that cause difficulty in breathing. Studies have also found that some 20% of healthy individuals are unusually sensitive to ozone, for no apparent reason. The only way to identify an ozone-sensitive person is to expose him or her to the pollutant.

Epidemiological studies of ozone exposure have been somewhat inconclusive. A study in southern Ontario, Canada, performed in the 1970s, found that hospital admissions for respiratory illness rose as levels of ozone, sulfur oxides, and sulfates in the air increased; it was not possible, however, to single out the effects of ozone. A study of children at a summer camp in Medham, New Jersey, following a serious ozone pollution incident in 1982 found a high incidence of impaired lung function. But a survey of four neighborhoods in Los Angeles in 1981 did not find any clear-cut pattern of ill health in high-ozone areas.

The health effects of carbon monoxide have been more clearly established. When inhaled, carbon monoxide impairs the blood's ability to deliver oxygen to bodily tissues; at high concentrations, it can be fatal. Animal studies have found that carbon monoxide levels slightly higher than the EPA-permitted maximum produce arrhythmias, irregular heartbeats that can trigger heart attacks. High levels of carbon monoxide are believed to be especially dangerous for people with heart disease as well as for those with respiratory problems. Also at greater risk from this pollutant are cigarette smokers, who already inhale significant amounts of carbon monoxide. Even small doses of carbon monoxide—at levels common in many cities—have been shown to impair mental performance.

The effects of nitrogen oxides are hard to single out from those of other air pollutants, but animal studies have linked lung damage and respiratory infections to this product of fossil fuel combustion. In addition, laboratory studies using human subjects suggest that nitrogen oxides can aggravate asthma. Epidemiological studies of the effects of these pollutants have not

Rush-hour traffic on the Los Angeles Downtown Interchange contributes to the heavy smog that obscures the city's skyline—and endangers its residents' health.

been conclusive, however, and some scientists now believe that nitrogen oxides are primarily damaging as contributors to ozone formation.

Sulfur dioxide can cause serious health problems, particularly in combination with particulates. Alone, sulfur dioxide gas can irritate the lungs and aggravate respiratory diseases such as bronchitis. It can also cause damage when it combines with water vapor to form sulfuric acid droplets. Sulfuric acid has been shown to be a powerful irritant of the respiratory tract of laboratory animals, although it has not been linked with permanent lung damage in either animals or humans.

More serious damage appears to result when sulfur dioxide combines with solid particles in air to form sulfates, which can damage lung tissue if inhaled. Reactions of sulfur dioxide with metal particulates can produce such toxic compounds as zinc ammonium sulfate, which is believed to have played an important role in the 1948 disaster in Donora, Pennsylvania. The U.S. Office of Technology Assessment estimates that sulfates and other particulates may cause 50,000 premature deaths in the United States every year.

Another air pollutant that poses a serious health hazard is lead, which can accumulate in the body over time and cause serious damage to the kidneys, immune system, blood-forming organs, and nervous system. Studies by Herbert Needleman of the University of Pittsburgh have associated even relatively low levels of lead in the blood with reductions in children's intelligence quotients. The children in greatest danger are those living in inner cities, where airborne concentrations of lead are highest. Fortunately, thanks to the growing use of catalytic converters in cars, use of lead in gasoline—the primary source of this pollutant in its airborne form—has decreased in the United States by 95% over the past 15 years. (Several European nations and Japan have also reduced the lead content of their gasoline.) Although atmospheric concentrations of lead have dropped sharply as a result, the metal

Schoolchildren in Mezibori, Czechoslovakia, wear respirator masks to avoid inhaling sodium dioxide, a pollutant trapped in the air over their town by a thermal inversion.

is still widely used in other products, especially paints, and the overall amount of lead in the environment remains a significant health hazard.

Many other airborne toxic chemicals also endanger human health, and although their effects are often not clearly established, concern about them is growing. A 1987 report by the Environmental Protection Agency estimated that U.S. industries release 2.6 billion pounds of hazardous pollutants, including 235 million pounds of carcinogens, or cancer-causing substances. Most of what is known about the health hazards of toxic compounds has been learned from incidents of on-the-job exposure to these substances. Vinyl chloride, for example, was identified as a carcinogen because plastics industry workers who were exposed to it had an unusually high incidence of cancer.

Although the amounts of toxic substances released to the open air are much smaller than those within a factory, people who work or live near chemical and other industrial plants are also at risk. Some specific regions of the United States appear to be especially high-risk danger areas. One is an 85-mile industrial zone running from Baton Rouge to New Orleans in Louisiana, where a fifth of the nation's petrochemicals (chemicals derived from petroleum or natural gas) are produced. There is an unusually high rate of several forms of cancer in this region. In the Kanawha Valley of West Virginia, where 13 major chemical plants are located, the incidence of respiratory cancers was more than 20% above the national average between 1968 and 1977. Studies are under way attempting to link toxic pollutants with cancer and other health problems in such exposed populations.

The EPA has used existing scientific data on the effects of air pollutants to develop an index that is used for health warnings during periods of heavy air pollution. The pollution standards index runs up to a value of 500. Anything above 100 is unhealthful. When the readings are between 100 and 200, persons with heart and lung diseases are told to reduce outdoor activities. When they measure between 200 and 300, the warning is extended to the general population. Any reading above 300 indicates hazardous conditions that could cause adverse symptoms in healthy people and the death of ill and elderly persons. The old and the ill are instructed to stay indoors on such days, with windows and doors closed. The same warning is given to everyone living in a polluted area if the index nears 500.

Between 1976 and 1987, according to this index, the number of days with hazardous air pollution levels declined sharply. Air pollutants still pose significant health hazards,

Emissions of cadmium, arsenic, lead, and zinc from the Asarco smelter plant in North Denver, Colorado, pose a cancer risk to people who live or work near the facility.

however. In 1988, for example, 1 out of 3 Americans lived in the approximately 100 U.S. cities where ozone levels frequently exceeded safe levels, the worst example being Los Angeles, generally considered the smog capital of the United States. Other cities with particularly severe air pollution include Milan, Italy; Athens, Greece; New Delhi, India; Beijing, China; São Paulo, Brazil; and Mexico City, Mexico, where the air is so bad that breathing it is roughly equivalent to smoking two packs of cigarettes a day.

Although statistics on the physical effects of air pollution are not easily calculated, an alarming related statistic is that between 1970 and 1986, deaths in the United States from chronic lung diseases rose 36%. The costs of air pollution in terms of health care and lost productivity in the United States alone have been estimated at more than $100 billion; the cost in human life is incalculable.

The nose, chin, and other features on this statue, which stands outside the Field Museum of Natural History in Chicago, are being obliterated by acid-rain-induced corrosion.

chapter 3

ENVIRONMENTAL AND
PROPERTY DAMAGE

Germans have traditionally treasured their forests. There
was nationwide concern, therefore, when evidence of widespread
tree damage in what was then West Germany began to emerge in
the 1980s. Surveys by government agencies found that needles of
coniferous (evergreen) trees such as fir and spruce were turning
yellow, falling out, or showing deformities. A survey in 1988
showed that trees in more than half of the forested regions of
West Germany were weakened or damaged. The primary cause
of the damage, according to the German Ministry of Food,
Agriculture, and Forestry, was air pollution—more specifically,
acid rain.

Acid rain began to emerge as a serious problem in the
late 1960s, when scientists in Scandinavia noticed a decline in
fish populations in their lakes. Not long afterward, American
researchers at the Hubbard Brook Experimental Forest in New
Hampshire found similar changes, accompanied by an increase in
the acidity of the waters there. In the 1970s, a number of studies
related not only declining fish stocks but also forest damage to

acid rain from urban and industrialized areas, often hundreds of miles away.

Acidity is measured on a pH scale that runs from 0 to 14 and that measures the concentration of hydrogen ions in a solution (an ion is any electrically charged particle). The more positively charged hydrogen ions (H^+) in a solution relative to negatively charged hydroxyl ions (OH^-), the more acidic it is and the lower is its pH; conversely, the fewer hydrogen ions relative to hydroxyl ions, the more alkaline and the higher the pH. Lemon juice, which is highly acidic, has a pH of just above 2. The pH of a tomato is 4.6. Distilled water has a pH of 7, or *neutral*—neither acidic nor alkaline. Baking soda, an alkaline compound, has a pH of 8.1; ammonia, which is very alkaline, has a pH of 11.5. Every point on the pH scale marks a tenfold change in the concentration of hydrogen ions; a solution with a pH measurement of 4 is 10 times more acidic than one with a pH of 5.

A slight degree of acidity in the environment is normal. Uncontaminated rainwater is usually slightly acidic (approximately pH 5.6) because carbon dioxide in the atmosphere dissolves in water, producing a weak solution of carbonic acid. Precipitation can also become more acidic temporarily because of such natural events as volcanic eruptions, which send large amounts of nitrogen oxides into the atmosphere, and forest fires and lightning flashes, which cause nitrogen and oxygen in the atmosphere to react and form nitric acids. Another source of nitrogen and sulfur compounds is decaying organic matter. These natural phenomena can all contribute to acid deposition, but the sulfur and nitrogen oxides produced by fossil fuel combustion are the primary villains of the acid rain story. As described earlier,

Acid rain is devastating forests throughout the world, particularly in areas downwind from industrial regions.

these pollutants are transformed in air into sulfuric and nitric acids and sulfate and nitrate salts, which may be airborne for many days but eventually fall to earth, where they cause considerable damage to trees, soils, lakes, and waterways.

A lake or waterway that is damaged by acid rain does not appear to be polluted. It looks pristine and sparkling clear, a beautiful appearance that is actually a sign of death. Excess acidity has killed plants and fish that are vulnerable to changes in pH. Once a lake's pH drops below 6, various small organisms begin to die. The entire food chain is then disrupted, threatening other species. Acidity can also affect fish reproductivity; trout, for example, have trouble reproducing once a lake's or river's pH drops below 5.5. At pH 3.5, virtually all aquatic organisms die off. Acids can also poison fish by leaching toxic metals such as aluminum and mercury into water. These contaminated fish pose a threat to humans as well, as do the leached metals themselves, which can contaminate public water supplies.

It is believed that acidic deposition does not kill trees outright but slowly weakens them, reducing their ability to withstand extreme cold or heat, insect attacks, and viruses. Acids leach nutrients such as calcium and potassium from the soils in which the trees grow and from the trees themselves; they can also release molecules of toxic metals normally bound up in soils, which can then damage tree roots. Spruce and fir trees appear to be most susceptible to damage from acid rain, especially those at high altitudes, which are often bathed in acidic clouds.

Some soils are better able to withstand acidic fallout than others because they contain more alkaline substances, such as limestone, that can neutralize, or buffer, acids. The same is true for lakes and waterways that lie over alkaline rock formations. This *buffering capacity* declines, however, with repeated exposure to acids.

Around the world, forests, lakes, and waterways are suffering from acid rain. Especially hard-hit regions include the eastern United States, particularly the Adirondack and Appalachian mountains; southeastern Canada; Scandinavia; central Europe; and southwestern China. Acid rain is also becoming a problem in many less industrialized nations, where large amounts of nitrogen oxides are released by the burning of *biomass*—wood and other plant matter used as fuel or burned to clear land.

In 1980, President Jimmy Carter called for what became a 10-year, $500-million study of acid rain, the National Acid Precipitation Assessment Program (NAPAP). A NAPAP report released in 1990 concluded that acid rain was doing significant damage, but not as much as many had thought. "The sky is not falling, but there is a problem that needs addressing," said James R. Mahoney, the director of the program.

Nationwide, the NAPAP report concluded, fewer than 1,200 U.S. lakes had been made completely uninhabitable by acid rain—about 4% of all the lakes in the country. Another 5% of lakes had suffered enough acidification to endanger some

Tall smokestacks release pollutants higher up in the air, where winds may carry them hundreds of miles from their source.

species. The percentage of damaged lakes was much higher in the six regions at greatest risk: 8% in the lowlands of New England, 56% in the northern Florida highlands, 10% in the Appalachians, 11% in parts of northern Wisconsin and Michigan, and a similar 11% in the mid-Atlantic coastal plain. In the southwestern third of the Adirondacks, the report found, more than a third of the lakes were acidified, but no damaged lakes were found elsewhere in the Adirondacks.

On an even more troubling note, the NAPAP report concluded that some of these regions had not originally been thought to be a problem. Even in remote areas of the world, far from industrial and automotive pollution sources, precipitation was more acidic than had been thought, with an average pH of 5 rather than the normal 5.6 that had been assumed. "No site in the world is at all times free from long-range transport of pollutants," the report said.

Acid rain may also be damaging crops, although it appears to do so primarily in conjunction with ozone, which has been more clearly linked to crop destruction. The 1990 NAPAP report concluded that air pollutants have reduced U.S. crop yields by 5% to 10%, with reductions ranging from less than 1% for sorghum and corn to 7% for cotton and soybeans, and more than 30% for alfalfa.

Many environmentalists believe the damage done by acid rain is worse than indicated in the NAPAP report. In 1988, for example, New York State's Environmental Conservation Department surveyed almost half of the 2,700 Adirondack lakes, most of them in the 6-million-acre Adirondack Park, an upstate wilderness area. Of the 1,245 lakes surveyed, the department found that almost one-fourth had a pH of 5 or below, a level at

Giant, open-topped plastic chambers containing soybeans and other plants dot fields in Beltsville, Maryland, where U.S. Department of Agriculture scientists are studying the effects of ozone and other air pollutants on various crops.

which almost no fish could survive. Another 19% of the lakes had a pH between 5 and 6 and were described as endangered. In its survey, NAPAP had concluded that only 10% of Adirondack lakes were acidified, but that study excluded small, vulnerable lakes smaller than 10 square acres, which were included in the state survey.

Another 1988 study by the Environmental Defense Fund (EDF), a private environmental organization, examined several eastern coastal areas, including Long Island Sound and Chesapeake Bay and its tributaries. The EDF report concluded that increasing acidification was a major threat to marine species in these aquatic ecosystems. Excess nitrogen from agricultural fertilizers and acidic rainfall were causing algal blooms, which cut off sunlight and reduce the oxygen content of these waters, endangering the plants and animals that live in them.

Other countries are reporting severe damage from acid rain. The Ontario Ministry of the Environment in Canada, for example, estimates that 48,000 lakes in that province are currently threatened by acid rain—much of which is attributed to emissions from industrial and power plants in the midwestern United States.

Similarly, many European countries suffering from acid rain—including Norway, Sweden, Switzerland, and the Netherlands—receive much of their pollution from other countries, frequently those in eastern Europe. Because acid rain respects no borders, international efforts at control are being made in Europe and elsewhere. In 1988, 25 industrialized nations, including the United States, signed an international protocol that would go into effect at the end of 1994 and would limit nitrogen oxide emissions to 1987 levels. The protocol marked the first U.S. agreement to an international acid rain control program. At the same time, a group of 12 western European nations agreed to reduce nitrogen oxide emissions by 30% over the following decade—an agreement that the United States did not join.

PROPERTY DAMAGE

The overall damage caused by acid deposition and other forms of air pollution is difficult to determine but clearly is enormous. According to the National Academy of Sciences, acid rain alone costs the United States at least $6 billion annually in environmental and agricultural damage. In addition, air pollutants are harming a variety of materials and structures. Sulfur dioxide and acid deposition can corrode and tarnish metals, erode stone and concrete, and discolor or weaken paper, fabrics, leather, and paints. As mentioned earlier, ozone can damage rubber and textiles.

Particulates are especially destructive, accelerating the corrosion caused by gaseous air pollutants and damaging precision-made machinery. Particles of soot and dirt can also soil clothing, windows, and buildings. Particulates are also the form of air pollution most responsible for reducing visibility, which can cause airplane crashes and other accidents—in addition to harming scenic views.

Air pollution is also causing monuments to deteriorate, erasing artwork and history in the process. In 1990, when Italian authorities finished their restoration of the Campidoglio, the magnificent Roman square designed by Michelangelo, they had to make a hard decision about one of its outstanding features, an ancient statue of the emperor Marcus Aurelius Antoninus. The government chose not to leave it in the square, out of fear of deterioration caused by air pollution. The statue was placed indoors, inside a clear plastic box, to protect it from Rome's destructive air.

Thousands of miles away, acid rain is doing the same sort of damage to the temples of the ancient Maya civilization of the Yucatán Peninsula and southern Mexico. Palenque, a Maya ceremonial site in southern Mexico, is 75 miles from the nearest oil field, and Chichén Itzá, an impressive collection of temples and pyramids, is 225 miles away, but acid precipitation from oil fields has caused more damage in the past few decades than the ancient stone structures experienced in the previous 1,500 years. The notoriously noxious exhaust fumes of Mexican tourist buses, which have none of the emission controls found on U.S. vehicles, add to the damage.

The corrosion of historical monuments by polluted air is also evident in Europe. In Athens, T. D. Skoulikidis, a Greek scientist, estimates that the Acropolis and other monuments of the classical era have deteriorated more since the end of World War II than in the previous 2,400 years. In India, the marble and

A heavy smog envelops downtown Leipzig, East Germany—now part of unified Germany. Environmental experts believe that more than $100 billion must be spent to repair the environmental damage caused by East German power plant emissions.

sandstone of the Taj Mahal are being eroded by acids from emissions believed to originate at a nearby oil refinery.

In the United States, acid rain has damaged 35,000 historic buildings and 10,000 monuments in the Northeast, according to the NAPAP report. For example, the 1,600 monuments and tablets in Gettysburg National Military Park are being eaten away by acid precipitation originating in the region's coal-burning plants. The lettering and designs on tablets and the features of statues are steadily disappearing, sometimes to such an extent that monuments are almost unrecognizable.

Efforts to clean the structures with commercial solutions and brushes have failed and have even added to the damage in some cases. The National Park Service now sometimes uses a technique that removes corrosion with a pressurized stream of walnut shells, then coats the monument with protective wax. The procedure must be repeated every 12 to 18 months, however, and is expensive, costing $80,000 at Gettysburg alone in 1990. Decisions about whether to spend large sums of money to save such artifacts are not easily made—it is difficult to put a price tag on history.

Clean air legislation enacted in the 1970s required industrial plants such as this copper smelter in Morenci, Arizona, to reduce emissions of sulfur dioxide.

L E G I S L A T I O N

Legislation is an essential part of the drive for clean air. It is also a battleground that pits environmentalists, who generally favor pollution control whatever the cost, against representatives of industry, who fight to prevent inroads into profits. Few would argue, however, that air pollution controls are not in the long-term interests of all the earth's inhabitants. Growing air pollution has prompted increasingly stringent clean air laws in recent decades, especially in the United States, Japan, and western Europe.

There are two approaches to air pollution control. One is to set limits on the amount of a pollutant that can be released in a given area, leaving it up to the polluters to choose the best way to meet those limits. The second approach is to require every source of pollution to install a given control technology—often the best that is available.

The first approach, referred to as setting *ambient,* or outdoor, air quality standards, is the most widely used, in the United States and worldwide. However, it is often difficult to determine both the concentrations of pollutants in the air and their sources. Also, some polluters evade controls by using devices such as tall smokestacks that send pollutants out of the control region. Consequently, the second strategy, setting *emission* standards, has been gaining favor. It has been applied both to automobiles, which have been required to meet strict exhaust emission limits in the United States since the 1970s, and to stationary sources such as power plants, which are frequently required to have the best available systems to remove sulfur and other pollutants from smokestack gas.

Some U.S. cities and states began passing clean air legislation as early as the 19th century, but major progress against air pollution did not begin until recent decades. New York City, for example, made large improvements in its air quality in the 1960s and 1970s by requiring the use of less-polluting low-sulfur coal and passing regulations that shut down most apartment house incinerators. A national policy was lacking, until the 1960s, when Congress began taking legislative action. Since then, the United States has been ahead of most other nations in clean air legislation.

THE 1970 CLEAN AIR ACT

Congress passed the first Clean Air Act in 1963. The measure called for a study of air pollution problems but accomplished little else. It was not until 1970 that Congress, in a major achievement, passed a sweeping Clean Air Act that let the government set and enforce standards to limit pollution. By no coincidence, 1970 also marked the first celebration of Earth Day; nationwide rallies in support of the environment were held on April 22 of that year, and a number of significant environmental measures were soon adopted.

Junior high school students march through the streets of Kirkwood, Missouri, protesting against air pollution on the first Earth Day, April 22, 1970.

On the first day of 1970, the National Environmental Policy Act (NEPA) became law, establishing national policies and goals for protecting the environment. The Clean Air Act became law on the last day of the year. At the same time, Congress created the Environmental Protection Agency to administer the Clean Air Act and other environmental laws. Officially, the Clean Air Act of 1970 was a set of amendments to NEPA. One amendment authorized the EPA to set national ambient air quality standards, based on considerations of health hazards and property damage. The EPA set standards for six pollutants: carbon monoxide, lead, nitrogen oxides, ozone, particulates, and sulfur oxides.

There are two kinds of air quality standards, both of which set maximum concentration levels for a pollutant. Primary standards are set to protect health, secondary standards to protect "economic values" (e.g., crops and buildings) and the environment. In practice, the distinction between the two kinds of air quality standards often blurs. The primary and secondary standards for ozone, for example, are identical.

Another 1970 amendment authorized the EPA to set standards for air pollutants that are not covered by the air quality standards but that can cause serious, irreversible illness or death. The standards limited emissions of each pollutant for individual sources, such as factories. The EPA used its authority to set standards for seven hazardous pollutants: asbestos, benzene, beryllium, arsenic, mercury, radioactive substances, and vinyl chloride.

A third part of the act instructed the EPA to set "source performance standards," based on existing technology, that would limit pollution emissions from prominent sources, notably automobiles, power plants, and factories. Congress wrote specific standards for auto emissions directly into the act, despite the protests of car manufacturers, who argued the new limits could not be achieved. The standards went into effect, however, and were in fact met.

It was a different story for power plant emissions. The EPA was told to take economic considerations into account in enforcing this part of the act because Congress did not want to see plants closed and people put out of work. The EPA did set standards for emissions of sulfur oxides, nitrogen oxides, and several other pollutants, but not very stringent ones.

The EPA enforces the clean air laws region by region. For monitoring purposes, the United States is divided into 242 air quality control regions. Each is judged by whether it achieves the limits set by the EPA for each pollutant. That judgment is made on the basis of readings from monitors that are set up across each region. If a single monitor in a region exceeds federal standards for a single pollutant for four days or more in three consecutive years, that region is considered out of compliance with EPA standards.

Ideally, air quality standards would be swiftly set and enforced and the air would quickly become clean. In the real world, progress is considerably slower, partly for economic reasons. Because of major energy conservation programs that followed the oil price increases of the 1970s, relatively few new power plants were built and federal regulations issued by the EPA allowed most older plants to continue operations with few or no added controls.

The Clean Air Act set 1975 as the deadline for the whole nation to meet the new air quality standards. That did not happen, and in 1977, Congress passed amendments that extended the deadline for achieving the primary standards to 1982 and requested that the secondary standards be enforced "as expeditiously as possible."

These and other 1977 amendments toughened the Clean Air Act in some ways and weakened it in others. The new legislation gave more responsibility to the states. Each state was required to submit a detailed proposal for controlling the six primary air pollutants. A state that did not comply could lose federal highway funds or be banned from constructing new power plants. Plants capable of emitting more than 100 tons of a regulated pollutant in the course of a year were required to get a construction permit from the state, the federal government, or both. If the region was achieving the emission limits for a given pollutant, the new plant had to install "the best available control technology," a requirement designed to avoid deterioration of air quality. If the region had emissions greater than what the EPA allowed, the new plant had to meet either the lowest emission rate that any state requires or the lowest rate that any plant of its type has achieved, a requirement that is tougher and more expensive than the "best available technology" standard.

These requirements proved to be hard to meet and unpopular with industry, and the EPA began to soften them. In 1979, the agency developed a "bubble policy" that made things easier for many industries. This new policy set overall goals not for individual sources but for groups of sources in specific areas, the imaginary "bubbles." A company could allow one plant to emit more than the permissible limit of a pollutant if it made a corresponding reduction at another source elsewhere within its bubble.

The arrival of the Reagan administration in 1980 meant a further loosening of regulations. The clean air law was not changed, but its enforcement was weakened—for example, new carbon monoxide car exhaust standards were delayed twice. As a result, air quality, which had been steadily improving, began to decline. In 1981, the National Commission on Air Quality, created by Congress to monitor progress in the battle against air pollution, estimated that only eight urban areas would violate federal standards by 1987. In fact, 90 areas surpassed federal limits for ozone and 40 violated the carbon monoxide standard in 1988. The Clean Air Act was to be revised in 1982, but political and economic pressures made that impossible. Congress renewed the law year by year, while negotiations began for a new Clean Air Act. After eight years of lobbying and bargaining, a set of sweeping amendments called the Clean Air Act of 1990 was passed by Congress and signed by President George Bush in November of that year.

The 1990 Clean Air Act broke new ground. For the first time, the law included provisions addressing the problems of acid rain and the threatened ozone layer. But the heart of the 1990 legislation consisted of new requirements that focused not only on national and regional standards but also on specific pollutants, specific sources, and specific regions.

One example of this new focus is the act's provisions regarding ground-level ozone, considered perhaps the leading urban pollutant. The 1990 amendment classifies U.S. cities into 6 categories according to the severity of their ozone problem and gives them anywhere from 3 to 20 years to meet federal standards. Areas with more serious problems are given more time to comply.

The new act covers ozone-forming pollutant sources ranging from automobiles to shipyards to dry cleaners—it even includes hairsprays and window-washing compounds. Areas with the worst air quality must implement the most severe emission control measures in the shortest time; areas with moderate problems are given more time and less stringent requirements.

The 1990 Clean Air Act also includes a list of 189 toxic compounds whose emissions must be reduced. It requires that the EPA publish a list of all major sources of these pollutants within a year and establish control-technology standards within two years. Regarding acid rain, the law seeks to reduce annual emissions of

In 1990, President George Bush (seated) signs into law new clean air legislation as a group of public officers, including EPA Administrator William Reilly (second from left), looks on.

sulfur oxides from the 20 million tons recorded in 1980 to 10 million tons, with the reductions starting in 1995 and continuing into the 21st century. Nitrogen oxide emissions will be cut by 2 million to 4 million tons annually. To enforce these rules, the EPA is given the power to impose fines of up to $200,000, with jail sentences for some violators.

The 1990 amendments give ample evidence of the bargaining that was necessary to get them passed. For example, plants in Illinois, Indiana, and Ohio are given more time to reduce sulfur oxide emissions than those elsewhere. In addition, the acid rain provisions allow utilities to buy and sell permission to pollute, within limits. This arrangement works as follows: A power plant gets a pollutant allowance based on its required emission reduction. If a plant cannot meet the target, it can buy an allowance from another plant whose emissions are below the set limit. There are bonus points for exceeding reductions by a given percentage and other provisions that give industry some of the flexibility that it wanted in meeting standards.

Even with these concessions to industry, however, the amendments represent a clear overall tightening of clean air requirements, a trend that is also being seen in other countries. Some nations are ahead of the United States. Switzerland and Austria, for example, now have the world's strictest auto emission regulations. But many countries are just beginning to address air pollution problems and to enact clean air legislation. Canada, for example, started a program to reduce sulfur oxide emissions in 1985 and in 1988 followed with new automobile emission standards essentially identical to those adopted in the United States years earlier.

Germany had virtually no air pollution regulations until the 1980s. That policy changed as awareness grew of the damage being done by acid rain to the country's forests. In 1983, the West German government instituted a program requiring every large power plant to install the best available sulfur control technology. The Germans also began to emphasize auto emission controls. The German pollution control effort is complicated by the fact that Germany must live within the rules set by the European Community (EC), a political and economic organization that includes all the leading western European countries. In 1988,

In Milan, Italy, a man and his dog wear antipollution masks while walking through the city on a day with extremely bad air quality.

West Germany began lobbying the European Community to adopt strict auto emission standards. In 1989, the EC adopted U.S.-style emission standards for small cars and agreed in principle to adopt similar standards for larger cars in the 1990s.

It is hoped that political changes under way in eastern Europe and the Soviet Union will lead to improved air pollution regulations in these nations. Economic hardships make costly clean air restrictions few and far between in Third World countries, although some initiatives have been taken. Brazil, for example, intends to have auto emission standards like those in the United States by the year 1997. In Mexico City, driving restrictions have been enacted and a large oil refinery has been shut down. Such initiatives, combined with assistance from more prosperous nations, may enable the poorer countries of the world to make some progress in the battle against air pollution.

THE COST OF CLEAN AIR

Clean air, and a clean environment in general, does not come cheap. A 1990 analysis by the EPA determined that the United States was spending about 2% of its approximately $5 trillion gross national product (GNP)—the total value of its goods and services—to control pollution and clean up the environment, about the same percentage as other major industrialized nations. The total cost of federally mandated pollution control and cleanup programs was put at $100 billion in 1990. This cost could rise to more than $150 billion by the year 2000, according to the EPA. Of the total 1990 budget, $26.7 billion was spent for clean air, an amount projected by the agency to rise to $44 billion by the year 2000.

Although the costs of pollution control may seem tremendous, environmentalists argue that they are small relative to the long-term costs of health and environmental damage caused by pollution. This toll is difficult to compute but is clearly enormous. The American Lung Association, for example, has calculated that the health care cost alone of air pollution in the United States is as much as $93 billion annually—more than is now spent on air pollution control.

Environmentalists are developing new kinds of accounting systems that attempt to take the costs of pollution into consideration. Currently, environmental damage is not subtracted when determining the GNP; in fact, it is sometimes added. When a new car is sold in the United States, for example, the cost of its emission control systems are included in the overall price of the automobile and considered an asset, or gain, to the GNP. Environmental economists argue for a national accounting system that would list such pollution control systems as a debit, or loss, to the GNP, because they are built to make up for the loss of clean air.

Another new accounting method factors depletions of natural resources into the GNP to produce what is called *gross sustainable productivity* (GSP). Congress has requested that the U.S. Commerce Department calculate this GSP in addition to the conventional GNP. A number of other nations are also moving toward such an environmental accounting system. France and Norway have begun to compile inventories of their natural resources as a step toward calculating environmental damage. The Dutch government has created a Department for Environmental Statistics to collect data on all pollutant emissions and environmental damage. The United Nations Statistical Commission is preparing guidelines for countries that want to prepare gross national product figures that include environmental impacts.

These new environmental accounting systems could be used to determine the most cost-effective ways to clean the air.

In formal economic terms, the issue is one of *internalizing* the costs of pollution, meaning that the cost of pollution control or pollution damage is paid by the polluter. Pollution costs are said to be *externalized* if the polluter pays for neither emission controls nor pollution damage. The manufacturer of an automobile with no emission controls, for example, or the owner of a generating plant without scrubbers to remove sulfur dioxide from its stack gases is said to externalize his or her costs—someone else pays for the damage. A car with a catalytic converter and a plant with a scrubber are said to have internalized pollution costs.

"Internalizing the environmental costs imposed on society by polluters is the wave of the future," Richard L. Ottinger of the Pace University Center for Environmental Legal Studies wrote in 1990. "By signalling to industry the true societal costs of their operations, inclusion of environmental costs in the price of goods produced gives an economic incentive to reduce pollution."

Several efforts have been made to calculate the overall dollar costs of specific air pollutants, Ottinger noted. Based on health effects, the cost of a pound of sulfur dioxide has been calculated at $2.03; the price of nitrogen oxides at 82 cents a pound; and particulates at $1.19 a pound. The estimates are imperfect, Ottinger noted, because many costs of pollution are not known or are difficult to evaluate; however, they are better than nothing. One way to internalize these costs is by imposing pollution taxes, based on the amount of emissions produced. Such taxes are being considered by several European countries. Another approach is to require utilities to include the cost of pollution in their operating estimates.

New economic tools for making these calculations are coming into use. At Johns Hopkins University in Baltimore, Maryland, for example, systems analyst Hugh Ellis has developed a computerized technique for applying what is called *cost-benefit analysis* to the problem of acid rain. To determine the point of greatest cost-effectiveness—where the least spending produces the greatest benefits—Ellis's computer compares the costs of reducing sulfur dioxide emissions with the costs of the environmental damage that will result if the emissions are not reduced.

An air monitoring station in Oklahoma City, Oklahoma—one of many such facilities nationwide—contains equipment that measures concentrations of various air pollutants.

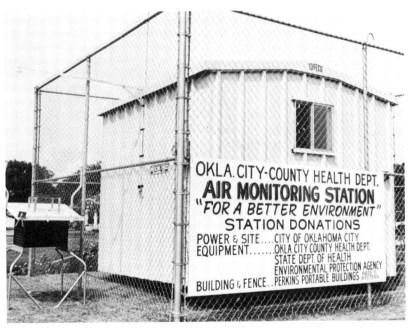

In one analysis, Ellis evaluated 230 emission sources over a large section of the country that ultimately cause acid rain damage in Maryland. He then used mathematical programming to determine how emissions from each of the sources could be reduced to eliminate acid rain damage at the lowest overall cost. Again, the technique is not perfect, because it requires the programmer to place specific dollar values on such things as a forest view or a national monument. But it is a starting point for the tough-minded economic decisions on air pollution control that lie ahead.

Larry Allen, a technician at the Pennsylvania Department of Transportation garage in Harrisburg, analyzes emissions from a truck's tail pipe as part of a statewide inspection program for vehicles in counties with high pollutant levels.

chapter 5

THE AUTOMOBILE

From one point of view, the automobile represents one of the great success stories in the fight against air pollution. The average 1991 model American car emits 96% less carbon monoxide, 96% fewer hydrocarbons, and 76% less nitrogen oxide than the auto of 1970. Unfortunately, increasing numbers of cars on the roads in the United States and around the world, as well as greater use of these cars, has offset these emissions reductions, and vehicle exhaust pollution remains a serious and growing problem.

Americans drove 50% more miles in 1990 than they did in 1970. More of those miles were in stop-and-go traffic, in which more pollutants are emitted. The increase in cars and miles driven has resulted in an increase in ozone-level violations. Between 1985 and 1988, for example, the number of metropolitan areas that did not meet the federal limit for ozone pollution rose from 64 to 101.

The automobile problem is also becoming a global concern. In 1988, the worldwide auto population rose to more than 400 million, with the greatest growth taking place in the newly industrialized nations of Asia, such as Korea and Taiwan.

Trucks included, there were 540 million motor vehicles on the planet as of 1991. The World Resources Institute estimates that the number will approach 1 billion early in the next century. Although sales are increasing in Europe, Japan, and the United States, the World Resources Institute predicts that the most rapid growth will continue to be in developing regions of Africa, Asia, and Latin America.

Most developing nations have few automobile exhaust controls. The situation is different in the industrialized nations. The United States has led the way in legislation to control auto emissions, followed closely by Japan, which now has rules as strict as those in the United States. There is increasing pressure for greater reductions in motor vehicle emissions in Europe, with demands for better control technology, new kinds of fuel, new commuting habits, and new kinds of automobiles.

EMISSION CONTROLS

The easiest of these demands to meet—if one is willing to pay the price—is requiring better emission controls on individual automobiles. The basic technology for reducing auto emissions came into use in 1975 and has improved steadily since then; it is based on the catalytic converter, which changes pollutants in exhaust gas into less harmful compounds.

Every American car made after 1975 has such a converter, which contains a catalyst such as platinum or palladium, both precious metals. A *catalyst* is something that speeds up a chemical reaction without being consumed in that reaction. In the automobile, the catalytic converter is involved in two completely different sets of reactions, both of which reduce pollution.

A researcher examines a porous silica bead under a magnifying glass. The beads can be used in auto-emissions control systems to improve energy efficiency.

The first reactions occur when a car engine is turned on. The temperature of the exhaust is relatively low, and the catalytic converter helps what are called oxidizing reactions, in which carbon monoxide reacts with air to form carbon dioxide while hydrocarbons react with air to form carbon dioxide and water. As the engine warms up, a more complex set of reactions, most of which involve nitrogen oxides, occurs in the converter. In these reactions, the nitrogen oxides are transformed into harmless nitrogen gas and ammonia. The ammonia undergoes further chemical reactions that form nitrogen gas and water.

The U.S. auto companies that fought the use of catalytic converters in the early 1970s now boast of their ability to mass-produce devices that perform these complex reactions reliably for 50,000 miles or more of driving. Over the years, the performance of catalytic converters has been improved by adding computerized sensor control systems and by making other changes in engines. The industry boasts that its newest vehicles are 26 times cleaner than the cars of the early 1970s.

That progress has not been good enough for California, where the city of Los Angeles still has the worst air pollution in the United States. The 12 million people living in the Los Angeles area rely almost entirely on motor vehicles for transportation. They live in an area that is bathed in sunlight most of the year and is surrounded by a ring of mountains. Weather and geography conspire to ensure the formation of photochemical smog—as sunlight transforms the chemicals from auto exhausts into ozone and other smog components—and to prevent its dispersion. (The same combination gives Mexico City infinitely worse air pollution because its valley contains more people and its motor vehicles do not have the emission controls found on American vehicles.) The Los Angeles Air Basin, as it is formally known, meets federal air standards for only two of six pollutants, sulfur dioxide and lead. It is the only area in the United States that does not meet the nitrogen dioxide standard. Carbon monoxide and particulate concentrations are double the legal maximum, and ozone concentrations are sometimes three times higher than the federal health standard.

California has thus become the driving force in the United States for ever-tighter air pollution controls covering every conceivable emission source. In 1990, the state Air Resources Board even proposed regulations that would require lawn mowers and other gasoline-driven garden machines to reduce emissions by 55%, starting in 1994. But the main focus of improvement has been on motor vehicles.

Since 1973, California has set tighter standards for automobiles than the other 49 states. In 1988, the South Coast Air Quality Management District, which has sweeping powers to regulate pollution in the Los Angeles Air Basin, adopted even stricter rules designed to bring the area into compliance with federal standards—but not before the year 2007 in the case of ozone and particulates. During the negotiations leading up to passage of the 1990 Clean Air Act, there was a major debate about whether the tough California automotive standards would be applied to the rest of the nation. To a great degree they were.

For example, the allowed emissions of hydrocarbons from all U.S. autos were lowered from 0.41 grams per mile to 0.25 grams per mile, and nitrogen oxide emission limits were lowered from 1 gram per mile to 0.4 grams. The EPA may cut those limits in half again by the year 2004 based on "need, feasibility and cost-effectiveness." The act also imposed a deadline, again based on California policy, on the introduction of less-polluting vehicles into the auto market. It requires that 30% of all new purchases by major car and truck fleets in 26 areas meet the toughest EPA standards, starting in 1998. The program could be delayed for three years if no vehicles being sold in California by that year meet the standards.

The new Clean Air Act also requires that 150,000 "clean fuel" (nongasoline) cars be sold in California in 1996 and 300,000 such cars in 1999. The toughest requirement is that beginning in 1998, 2% of the cars sold in California must emit no pollutants at all; that percentage must rise to 10% by the year 2003.

Some of the pollution reductions needed to meet these ambitious goals would be achieved by improving catalytic converter performance. The act requires that converters work for at least 100,000 miles, instead of the previous 50,000-mile guarantee. More progress would be made as older cars wear out and are replaced by newer models—the 1.2 million older cars and trucks in the Los Angeles area constitute only 15% of the vehicles there, but they emit more than 30% of the air pollutants. Other new pollution-reduction features will include canisters to capture gasoline vapors that evaporate when fuel is pumped into the tank; better electronic emission monitors; and pumps that recycle exhaust gas through the engine to reduce emissions.

Petroleum companies have begun developing lower-emission gasoline. The ARCO Corporation was the first, introducing a lead-free, less-polluting fuel in the Southern California market in 1989. ARCO's fuel contains an additive called methyl tertiary butyl ether (MTBE) that contains extra oxygen, which promotes better combustion. It also contains lower amounts of those hydrocarbons most likely to react in sunlight to form smog. According to ARCO, its fuel reduces emissions of carbon monoxide by 10%, nitrogen oxides by 6%, and hydrocarbons by 5%. A number of other major oil companies have since followed ARCO's lead.

Another strategy for reducing vehicle exhaust pollution is the development of nongasoline fuels. One alternative fuel is alcohol, either ethanol (made from grain) or methanol (made from wood). Brazil has had an active alcohol fuel program for years. Large numbers of cars in that country run on fuel that is 22% ethanol made from sugarcane.

In the United States, some alcohol is used as automobile fuel in the form of *gasohol,* a blend of 90% gasoline and 10% ethanol. Auto makers are cautious about increasing the percentage of alcohol because they say it could harm existing engines. They also note that alcohol has only half the energy content of gasoline, so drivers would have to refuel more often. Nevertheless, a large-scale program to test alcohol fuels has begun in California. In late 1990, the California Energy Commission launched a plan to manufacture several thousand automobiles with engines modified to burn any mixture of gasoline and methanol.

Another alternative fuel already in use is compressed natural gas. This fuel now powers more than 30,000 vehicles in the United States, mostly delivery trucks and school buses. Natural gas costs less than gasoline and emits fewer hydrocarbons and less carbon monoxide. However, it emits more nitrogen oxides, and its use requires bulkier tanks. Vehicles powered by this fuel also have a shorter range than gasoline-powered cars and trucks. Natural gas is cheaper than gasoline, however, and the

The Ford Motor Company's Flexible Fuel Vehicle (FFV) can burn methanol, gasoline, or a combination of these two fuels in the same tank. The FFV is intended as a provisional alternative-fuel vehicle until more methanol refueling stations are built.

American Gas Association, an industry trade group, says it more than repays the estimated $2,500 conversion cost for a car or truck engine.

In 1990, the 3 major American automobile manufacturers, the Ford Motor Company, the General Motors Corporation, and the Chrysler Corporation, joined with 14 oil companies in a program to evaluate these and other alternative fuels. Results from their studies are not expected for several years.

ELECTRIC CARS

Another possible solution to the car exhaust problem is the electric car, which emits no pollution and does not even have an exhaust pipe. Electric cars have not been competitive for many decades because their batteries cannot store enough energy to

A mechanic inspects the batteries of an electric car designed by Electric Vehicle Associates of Ft. Belvoir, Virginia. The automobile's batteries require eight hours to recharge after they have been 80% discharged.

give them sufficient range (the distance that can be traveled without refueling), speed, and acceleration. Several major automobile companies have been trying to develop better batteries, but the results have not yet been very impressive. For example, ABB, a Swedish-Swiss engineering group, has developed a sodium-sulfur battery that stores four times more energy than the lead-acid batteries used in today's autos. ABB's invention is being tested by Volkswagen in Germany for use in commuter cars, which are generally used to travel shorter distances at lower speeds. The battery is expensive, however, and requires a special cooling system because it operates at temperatures above 500 degrees Fahrenheit.

In the United States, General Motors has developed an electric car called the Impact. The car seats 2 people, has a range of 120 miles, and is powered by 32 conventional lead-acid batteries, which must be replaced after 20,000 miles. The energy cost of the Impact is twice that of a gasoline-fueled car. In Italy, Fiat has an electric car called the Elletra, also using lead-acid batteries, that is being proposed as a city car. It has a top speed of 45 miles per hour and a range of 60 miles.

Several auto companies are experimenting with hybrid cars that use a combination of batteries and a conventional internal combustion engine. Volkswagen has a model that runs on electricity but uses a small diesel engine for extra range and acceleration. Toyota has an electric car that includes an internal combustion engine to charge the battery, extending the car's range. These models have much lower emissions than do gasoline-powered vehicles.

Even if there is a breakthrough in battery technology, electric cars present several problems. One is recharging the battery, a procedure that currently takes six to eight hours. Widespread use of electric cars would probably necessitate building public recharging centers where owners could plug in. Electric cars also cost more to run than gasoline-powered models. Because of these drawbacks, government subsidies or other policies are needed to promote the use of electric cars. The California law calling for a growing percentage of nonpolluting cars starting in 1998 is one such policy; it creates a potential market of 180,000 vehicles early in the next century.

Another problem with electric cars is that although they do not emit air pollutants themselves, they rely on electricity from fossil-fuel-fired power plants that are currently not themselves pollution-free.

DRIVING RESTRICTIONS

Several unusual new strategies for reducing pollution from vehicles involve restrictions on driving, a policy even more controversial than new emission control technology and alternative fuels because it infringes on what many people regard

Automatic sensors have been installed in parts of Kiev and other Soviet cities to control air pollution. The sensors are linked to traffic lights that stop motor vehicles from entering areas with excessively high air pollutant levels.

as their natural right to drive anywhere at any time. These restrictions include taxation and outright bans on driving.

In Singapore, for example, drivers are charged five dollars a day for a special license plate that allows them to enter the city in the morning. The system has cut morning traffic by 60%. In Mexico City, the government has prohibited each of the city's 2.5 million cars and small trucks from being used one day of every workweek, a regulation that keeps about half a million cars off the streets every business day. High fines help prevent violations of this rule, although many drivers have resorted to purchasing second cars to evade the restriction, and growing numbers of cars in the city combined with increasing industrialization continue to create terrible smog there.

The university city of Cambridge, England, is examining a program that would charge motorists for the congestion they cause. Every vehicle in the area would get a meter that would be switched on automatically as the car enters the city by a set of beacons set around the city limits. Drivers would pay fees based on the slowness of traffic, which would be recorded on the basis of the car's stop-and-go pattern of driving. The major purpose of the plan is to reduce congestion, but it would also reduce air pollution. The technology to implement such a program already exists in the United States, where radio-based transmitters attached to automobiles are used to collect bridge and road tolls in Dallas, Texas and New Orleans, Louisiana.

Granular-bed filters such as this one are used in a pressurized fluidized bed combustor system to reduce pollutant emissions in coal-burning plants.

C L E A N   E L E C T R I C I T Y

The percentage of total U.S. energy consumption used to generate electricity grew from 27% in 1973 to 36% in 1989. In that year, nearly 56% of the nation's electricity was generated by coal-burning plants; nuclear plants accounted for another 19%, hydroelectric and natural gas sources for 9.5% each, and oil for 5.7%, with a small fraction from other sources. The United States will continue to burn a lot of coal because it constitutes the major part of the nation's fuel reserves. At the present rate of consumption, the United States has enough coal reserves to last nearly two centuries, far longer than U.S. reserves of oil or natural gas. The challenge in an era when clean air is increasingly important is to burn coal with a minimum of pollution.

As mentioned earlier, coal contains varying amounts of sulfur. There are also two kinds of sulfur in coal. *Organic* sulfur is chemically bonded to coal molecules, whereas *pyritic* sulfur is separate. Pyritic sulfur can be physically removed from coal; organic sulfur cannot.

When the U.S. Clean Air Act of 1970 set maximum limits on sulfur emissions from power plants, most facilities were able to comply with the law by burning low-sulfur coal. That situation changed when the 1977 Clean Air Act amendments imposed much stricter limits on plants built after 1978, requiring them to reduce sulfur emissions by an additional 70%. Power plants have employed several techniques to meet these new limits. These improvements are being used more extensively, and new methods are being tested, to meet the much more demanding goals set by the Clean Air Act of 1990.

One method of limiting sulfur pollution is to clean coal before it is burned. About 40% of U.S. power plant coal is cleaned, usually by crushing and washing it to remove particles of pyritic sulfur. Existing methods take out 30% to 50% of pyritic sulfur. Experimental methods can remove even more by using chemical techniques, such as exposing the coal to a hot sodium compound that leaches out the sulfur. Another intriguing new method under development uses bacteria that literally eat pyritic and organic sulfur.

Coal can also be cleaned as it is burned. The conventional combustion method is to crush coal into tiny particles that are then blown into a furnace. Several techniques are being developed to remove sulfur during combustion. One promising method mixes crushed coal with limestone and uses jets of air to suspend the mixture in the boiler. The sulfur that is released as the coal burns is absorbed by the limestone, which combines with it chemically. *Fluidized bed combustion,* as this procedure is called, can trap up to 90% of the sulfur, reduce carbon dioxide emissions by 20%, and increase energy efficiency. Invented in Germany, this combustion method is now widely used in smaller plants and is expected to be installed in larger plants starting in the mid-1990s.

Two forms of fluidized bed combustion are available. In one method, the burning takes place at atmospheric pressure—the pressure of air at sea level, or 14.7 pounds to the square inch. In pressurized fluidized bed combustion, the boiler pressure is made 10 times or more higher than atmospheric pressure. The pressurized method removes more sulfur from emissions and also increases the efficiency of the plant—that is, the amount of electricity it obtains from a given amount of fuel—by up to 50%.

Several other methods of sulfur removal during combustion are being tested. One involves injecting an absorbing compound, or sorbent, into the furnace, where it combines with sulfur. Another uses a *slagging combustor*, which operates at such a high temperature that the mineral matter in coal melts into slag (the refuse from melting of metals), in which the sulfur is trapped.

In existing generating plants, most sulfur removal is done after combustion, as gas goes up the smokestack. The basic postcombustion sulfur-removing device is called a *scrubber*, which comes in two forms, wet and dry. A wet scrubber sprays a combination of water and crushed limestone into the stack gas. This limestone slurry combines chemically with the sulfur to form a wet sludge that is about as gooey as toothpaste. The best wet scrubbers remove more than 90% of sulfur. The plant is left with the problem of disposing of the sludge, which usually is put into a disposal pond. A 500-megawatt plant will produce enough sludge in its lifetime to fill a 500-foot pond to a depth of 40 feet. (A megawatt is 1 million watts of electricity.) Another drawback of wet scrubbers is that they use up to 8% of a plant's energy output, reducing its efficiency.

It is possible to get usable products from wet scrubbers. The Japanese, who do not have the land for sludge disposal ponds and operate under much stricter environmental regulations than U.S. utilities, use a method that produces usable gypsum instead of sludge. The Japanese use the substance to make plasterboard. Japan's many scrubbers have cut sulfur dioxide emissions there by more than 70%. That country also has an aggressive program of fuel desulfurization that reduced the average sulfur content of its fossil fuels from 1.5% in 1970 to 0.28% in 1989.

A dry scrubber injects a fine mist of limestone particles into the stack gas. Water in the mist evaporates, leaving behind only dry particles that contain the sulfur. Dry scrubbers pose less of a sludge disposal problem but are more expensive and less effective than wet scrubbers and produce large amounts of hazardous scrubber ash.

Another method for reducing sulfur dioxide emissions is to convert coal into clean-burning gas. Even though gas conversion can remove up to 99% of sulfur, it is not a widely used method because of its relatively high cost. In the 1970s, the Carter administration began a major coal-gasification program to reduce U.S. dependence on imported oil. The federal program came to an end under the Reagan administration, when oil prices dropped sharply and coal conversion could not compete economically.

Very small particulate matter can be removed from exhaust gases by such devices as the *baghouse filter*, a vacuum-cleaner–like apparatus that traps particle emissions in fabric filters. Tiny particulates can also be trapped using an *electrostatic precipitator*, which pulls electrically charged pollutant particles

This coal-liquefaction facility converts solid coal into oil, which can then be refined to produce synthetic gasoline. The resulting fuel is less polluting than coal, but the procedure is expensive and has a low energy yield.

out of the exhaust stream onto a screen with the opposite charge.

Reduction of nitrogen oxide emissions requires different strategies than those used to reduce sulfur emissions. Although some nitrogen in coal forms polluting oxides during combustion, most nitrogen oxides are produced when the high temperatures inside a boiler cause nitrogen and oxygen in the air to combine, something that does not happen at lower temperatures. Nitrogen oxides present a dilemma: High combustion temperatures achieve greater energy efficiency, but they also result in the formation of more of this pollutant.

One solution to this problem is to modify the combustion process so that fuel and air are mixed more gradually, which lowers the boiler temperature. Another method is to adjust the fuel mix so that there is just enough oxygen to support combustion without forming nitrogen oxides. In another technique, air ports are put into the furnace wall above the burners to create a fuel-rich region where little nitrogen oxide can form. All these methods are only partially effective, cutting nitrogen oxide formation by 15% to 50%. It is also possible to reduce nitrogen oxide emissions by injecting ammonia into the smokestack, where it combines chemically with nitrogen oxides to form ordinary nitrogen gas and water.

A worker at the Aluminum Company of America's plant in Wenatchee, Washington, installs baghouse filters that remove aluminum and coke dust particles from the plant's furnace emissions.

Another technique for reducing both sulfur and nitrogen oxide pollution is to burn natural gas with coal. Use of natural gas in generating plants was considered wasteful in the 1970s because supplies appeared to be limited. New supplies have become available since then, however, and the United States now has a gas surplus. Natural gas burns cleanly, emits almost no sulfur dioxide, and, burned properly, can reduce nitrogen oxide emissions.

One method under study is *cofiring*, in which coal and natural gas are burned simultaneously in the same boiler. Separate burners are used for each fuel and are generally placed at different heights in the boiler. Sulfur dioxide emissions are reduced in direct proportion to the amount of gas that is burned: If 10% of the fuel is natural gas, 10% less sulfur dioxide is emitted. Nitrogen oxide emissions are also reduced.

Reburning is a technique aimed primarily at reducing nitrogen oxide emissions. Coal is burned in the lower part of a boiler, providing 80% to 90% of the energy. Natural gas is added in a "reburn" region higher in the boiler. Hydrocarbons in the natural gas combine chemically with nitrogen oxides produced by coal combustion, producing ordinary, harmless nitrogen gas. A gas reburning system can reduce nitrogen oxide emissions by 40%. Reburning can be combined with sorbent injection to reduce emissions even further.

Bringing highly polluting power plants into conformity with the Clean Air Act of 1990 is a major concern of electric utilities. The acid rain provisions of the act are aimed primarily at power plants, which emit most of the 20 million tons of sulfur dioxide put into the air yearly by combustion. The act requires that these sulfur emissions be cut in half, with a permanent limit of 8.9 million tons effective in the year 2000. Utilities must meet these limits and at the same time satisfy a steadily increasing demand for more electricity. They must also comply with demands for reduced emissions of carbon dioxide because of fears of global warming.

A major issue is whether older power plants exempted under the 1970 Clean Air Act should now be fitted with scrubbers. Although the United States has more than half of the scrubbers installed worldwide, a majority of U.S. generating plants do not have these devices. Electric utilities claim that installing scrubbers on older plants would exceed the original cost of the plants and would take money away from research programs devoted to developing clean coal technologies.

The electric power industry has an active research program run by an organization called the Electric Power Research Institute, with the participation of many individual utilities. This research is done in collaboration with the U.S. Department of Energy, which began a $5 billion clean coal technology program in 1989, with half the money to come from the government and the other half from private sources.

Several dozen research projects using all the technologies described above are now under way. The success of these projects is vital to the success of the latest Clean Air Act. Utilities are responsible for 9 million tons of the 10-million-ton reduction in sulfur dioxide emissions mandated by the act. The Edison Electric Institute estimates the cost of building and installing the equipment needed to meet the new sulfur dioxide and nitrogen oxide standards at $18.8 billion by the year 2004. The same organization's estimates of annual operating costs for sulfur and nitrogen oxide pollution control start at $4 billion a year. Nationwide, the average utility bill will go up an average of 2.5% but may rise as much as 10% to 15% in some states— and that just to meet the demand for acid rain reductions. As electricity consumption grows, however—in the United States, for example, at a predicted annual rate of 2.4%—and more coal is burned, new emission-reduction technologies will become necessary to prevent ever greater and more destructive amounts of air pollution.

An eye-stinging, lung-irritating smog envelops New York City on a hot summer day. Increasing fossil fuel combustion in motor vehicles, power plants, and various industrial processes threatens to worsen both urban and rural air pollution in the coming decades.

A   N O N P O L L U T I N G
F U T U R E

The main clean air strategy for the past few decades
has been to burn fuel more cleanly, thus reducing pollutant
emissions. The Clean Air Act of 1990 continued that strategy.
But other approaches, including developing alternative energy
sources, are now coming more into play—and not for reasons of
clean air alone. Many scientists predict that the temperature of
this planet will soon rise because of global warming, caused in
large part by the burning of fossil fuels. Some believe that such
a warming is already under way.

Another argument for pursuing alternative energy sources
is that supplies of fossil fuels, although adequate for the present,
will run out eventually—probably within a few hundred years.
What are needed, therefore, are energy production technologies
that will last longer and also emit less pollution and fewer
greenhouse gases into the atmosphere.

Nuclear energy, the most immediately available of
these technologies, is also the most controversial. Today's
nuclear power plants derive energy from the heat released by
the *fissioning,* or splitting, of atoms, the smallest characteristic

components of the elements from which all substances are made. More than 30 countries worldwide currently meet some of their energy needs using nuclear fission. In 1990, nuclear power plants provided nearly 20% of U.S. electricity. In France, that figure is 75%; in Korea, 50%; and in Japan, 30%.

There are some advantages to nuclear power. Under ordinary circumstances, nuclear power plants do not emit large amounts of air pollutants or carbon dioxide, although some air pollution is created in the mining of uranium, the fuel needed to produce nuclear energy. Another advantage to nuclear power is that there are sufficient uranium supplies worldwide to last hundreds of years longer than fossil fuels—possibly thousands of years if the technology for *breeder* reactors that produce more fuel than they consume is perfected. (A reactor is a device in which the fission reaction takes place.)

Several major controversies have brought the U.S. nuclear power program to a virtual standstill—no new generating plants have been ordered since the 1970s—and have stalled the industry elsewhere in the world as well. One of the serious drawbacks to nuclear power is the potential for radiation-releasing accidents such as those that occurred at the Three Mile Island plant in Pennsylvania in 1979 and at Chernobyl in the Soviet Union in 1986. The Chernobyl accident contaminated thousands of square miles of the Soviet Union and sent a cloud of radioactivity across Europe and even farther, with a human toll that has yet to be calculated.

Defenders of nuclear energy point out that the Chernobyl plant used a design that was rejected as unsafe in the United States and that, unlike U.S. plants, it did not have a containment structure to help prevent the release of large amounts of radio-

Nuclear power is normally less polluting than traditional energy sources such as coal, but it creates a number of other hazards, including the potential for radiation-releasing accidents.

activity. Nevertheless, some officials at the Nuclear Regulatory Commission estimate that there is a 45% chance of a Chernobyl-scale accident happening in the United States by the year 2000, and the chance that one will happen somewhere else in the world even sooner is higher.

The nuclear industry argues that a new generation of better-designed reactors with improved safety features will be both safer and less expensive than those now in use. The U.S. Council for Energy Awareness, a nuclear industry group, estimates that these new plants will generate power at 4.6 cents per kilowatt-hour, compared to their estimates of 5 cents for coal-fired plants and 8.2 cents for oil-burning plants. Newer U.S. nuclear power plants now in use, by contrast, generate electricity at an average cost of more than 13 cents per kilowatt-hour.

Even if nuclear power plants of the future are safer and cheaper, several other problems remain to be solved, including that of nuclear waste disposal. The ever-growing amounts of radioactive waste from nuclear fission remain dangerous for many thousands of years, and storing them safely is proving extremely difficult, if not impossible. Another major drawback to nuclear fission is its potential diversion for nonpeaceful purposes. Both the plutonium produced by nuclear power plants and the plants themselves may be used for nuclear weapons production.

Another potential energy source is a type of nuclear energy called *fusion*. A fusion plant would produce energy by fusing atoms of hydrogen, duplicating a reaction that occurs in the sun and other stars. Plans are under way in the United States to build first a demonstration fusion plant and then a commercial plant, at a cost of several billion dollars. Fusion technology has not yet been perfected, however, and the commercial plant could not go into operation before the year 2040 at the earliest. There is considerable doubt as to whether this form of nuclear energy will ever be a practicable source of power.

Another energy solution—and the one most advocated by environmentalists—is to develop renewable energy sources such as solar power. The term *solar power* refers to a variety of technologies for turning the heat of the sun into electricity or other kinds of usable energy. Loosely speaking, the term includes technologies that derive energy from the sun indirectly. Alcohol fuel for automobiles, for example, comes from vegetation that grows by capturing solar energy. Only a relatively small number of solar facilities are in use today, most of them for specialized purposes. But proponents believe a well-funded research program can make solar energy technologies economically competitive.

Solar water heating is now in widespread use in hot, sunny countries, including Israel and Cyprus. An estimated 1 million solar heaters have also been built in the United States. They are simple in design: Water for household use is heated as it flows through rooftop pipes that expose it to the sun. Many such heaters were built after the Arab oil embargo of the 1970s, when oil prices moved up sharply and federal tax incentives were offered to encourage solar power development. The industry

The Tokamak Fusion Test Reactor at the Princeton Plasma Physics Laboratory in Princeton, New Jersey. Nuclear fusion is a potentially huge energy source but may prove too expensive and impracticable.

went into a decline, however, when oil prices dropped and the tax incentives were ended.

Another form of solar energy uses *photovoltaic* cells, which convert energy from sunlight directly into electricity. The federal Solar Energy Research Institute estimated the cost of photovoltaic electricity in 1988 at 30 cents per kilowatt-hour, against 5 to 10 cents for coal-fueled generating plants. The organization forecast a drop to 10 cents per kilowatt-hour by the year 2000 and 4 cents by 2030, as improvements in photovoltaic technology are expected to reduce production costs as well as increase efficiency.

The largest photovoltaic plant in operation as of 1990 was a 6.5-megawatt facility operated by Pacific Gas and Electric in California. Built in 1983, the plant uses motors to keep solar panels turned toward the sun as it moves across the sky. Europe's biggest photovoltaic plant is a 340-kilowatt system in a former vineyard near Koblenz, Germany.

Wind power is often classified as solar energy, because winds are produced as the heat of the sun acts on the atmosphere. About 80% of the world's wind-produced electricity is generated in California, in vast wind-turbine farms that cover thousands of acres in suitably windy regions. More than 15,000 wind turbines were installed in California in the 1980s, under the stimulus of federal and state tax incentives; collectively they generate more than 1,500 megawatts of electricity annually. The growth of this industry has continued since the incentives stopped because the best wind turbines now generate electricity for less than 7 cents per kilowatt-hour, which makes them competitive with fossil fuel plants. Advanced wind turbines expected to produce electricity for 5 cents per kilowatt-hour are under development.

Other nations are developing this technology as well, including Denmark and several other European countries; it is estimated that Europe will have 2,000 to 4,000 megawatts of wind-generated electricity by the end of the 1990s.

Another alternative energy source is *hydropower,* or the generation of electricity from falling water, a process that currently supplies about 20% of the world's electricity. Most hydropower projects use large dams built across rivers; water is released from the dam at a controlled rate to spin electricity-generating turbines. The United States obtains about 10% of its electricity from this source; Canada, more than 70%. A number of large hydropower projects are planned or are under way in developing nations. Dam-building does not create air pollutants. However, the flooding it produces can disrupt aquatic ecosystems and wildlife habitats, cause soil erosion and water pollution, and displace large numbers of people.

Geothermal energy technology uses heat from within the earth's crust to heat water or buildings or to generate electricity. Wells can be drilled to extract steam or hot water from underground deposits; another approach uses pumps to obtain heat from hot subsurface rocks. The United States is the largest producer of geothermal energy. Worldwide, this energy source supplies electricity equivalent to that produced by about five large coal-burning plants. This form of energy is abundant and inexpensive and releases no carbon dioxide. However, the water from geothermal deposits sometimes contains harmful salts and minerals; it can also release significant amounts of hydrogen sulfide, radioactive materials, and other air pollutants.

The world's oceans are another potential energy source. Several methods of converting the energy of the seas into usable

At Solar One, a solar power plant in the Mojave Desert, about 1,800 giant movable mirrors reflect sunlight onto a central tower that produces steam to generate electricity.

power are being explored. One uses underwater turbines driven by wave power. The Norwegian government operated two small wave power plants for a time in the 1980s. Another technique is to build turbines that intercept waves as they run back out to sea. One such generating station is operating in Great Britain.

For decades, there has been ambitious talk about capturing the energy of the tides. To date, the only tidal power facility in operation is in France, at the river Rance in Brittany. It was designed to be the prototype for a much larger project, but the French government chose instead to build more nuclear plants. Drawbacks to both wave and tidal power plants include a scarcity of appropriate locations for these facilities and the potential for damage from storms and corroding seawater.

Another alternative energy proposal would link solar energy to a fuel that is almost nonpolluting, is potentially available in limitless amounts, and can be used to replace oil when it runs out. The fuel is hydrogen, which combines with oxygen when it burns to produce pure water. Hydrogen has a high energy content and is used in liquid form as a fuel in the space shuttle. It is obtained from natural gas at a cost more than four times that of gasoline. If hydrogen could be obtained at a reasonable cost by passing electricity through water, a process called electrolysis, it could be the fuel of the future.

At present, however, the best methods for extracting hydrogen from water make it at least five times more expensive than gasoline. The Germans have built a photovoltaic plant in Bavaria that uses electricity from solar cells to run an electrolyzer, a device that splits water into hydrogen and oxygen. It is hoped that the cost of photovoltaic electricity will continue to decrease and that hydrogen produced using this form of solar power will become economically competitive with gasoline in the 21st century.

Some hydrogen-powered cars are already on the road in Europe. They were built by Daimler-Benz, the Germany company best known for its Mercedes automobiles, and are fueled by liquid hydrogen. The cars illustrate the difficulties that complicate the vision of a hydrogen-fueled economy. Liquid hydrogen must be kept at more than 400° below zero, which necessitates using heavy, insulated tanks and special storage facilities for refueling. These requirements limit the usefulness of liquid hydrogen. Another possibility is to use hydrogen in the form of hydrides, compounds that release hydrogen readily. Unfortunately, existing hydrides do not hold enough hydrogen to fuel automobiles for a reasonable number of miles. Researchers are working to develop better hydrides.

Another possible energy source using hydrogen involves combining it with oxygen in fuel cells, a technique currently used in spacecraft to generate electricity with high efficiency and almost no pollution. In a fuel cell, hydrogen and oxygen are separated by a barrier that allows them to combine under controlled conditions, generating an electric current. The best fuel cells are 70% efficient—nearly twice as good as conventional power plants—and are virtually nonpolluting.

Delegates to an international conference on environmental problems are given a dramatic reminder of the seriousness of the dilemmas they face.

Fuel cells have been held back by their high cost, but that is changing. In 1990, the U.S. electric utility industry began a program to develop a 2-megawatt fuel cell intended for use in cities. Utilities would like to have such small, nonpolluting plants because they could be built quickly and at relatively low cost very near the customers who would use the electricity. The fuel cell would use natural gas as its source of hydrogen; one thought is to get the fuel from the methane (the main constituent of natural gas) given off by garbage in landfills, solving another environmental problem.

Further technological advances are clearly needed for the world to have adequate supplies of nonpolluting energy in the future. If clean air is to be achieved, fossil fuels such as coal must be burned more cleanly and efficiently while they last and less polluting fuels must be developed. In addition, more regulation of toxic chemical emissions is needed. These goals are becoming more urgent as growing industrialization and energy consumption threaten to worsen air pollution and further endanger human health and the environment. If individual nations and the global community all take serious action to stop air pollution and find more nonpolluting energy sources, however, the earth may yet have enough energy—and a clean environment with clean air as well.

A P P E N D I X : F O R M O R E
I N F O R M A T I O N

Acid Rain Foundation
1630 Blackhawk Hills
St. Paul, MN 55122
(919) 828-9443

Air Pollution Control Association
P.O. Box 2861
Pittsburgh, PA 15230
(412) 578-8111

American Gas Association
1515 Wilson Blvd.
Arlington, VA 22209
(703) 841-8600

American Lung Association
1740 Broadway
New York, NY 10019
(212) 315-8700

Asthma and Allergy Foundation
   of America
1302 18th Street NW
Washington, DC 20036
(202) 265-0265

Canadian Coalition on Acid Rain
112 St. Clair Avenue West
Toronto, Ontario M4V 2Y3
Canada
(416) 968-2135

Center for Clean Air Policy
444 North Capitol Street/526
Washington, DC 20001
(202) 624-7709

Edison Electric Institute
1111 19th Street NW
Washington, DC 20036
(202) 778-6660

Electric Power Research Institute
P.O. Box 10412
3412 Hillview Avenue
Palo Alto, CA 94303
(415) 855-2000

Environmental Defense Fund
257 Park Avenue South
New York, NY 10010
(212) 505-2100

Environmental Protection Agency
401 M Street SW
Washington, DC 20460
(202) 382-2080
EPA radon hot line:
(800) 334-8571

Greenpeace USA
1436 U Street NW
Washington, DC 20009
(202) 462-1177

National Clean Air Coalition
530 Seventh Street SE
Washington, DC 20003
(202) 543-8200

National Coal Association
1130 17th Street NW
Washington, DC 20036
(202) 463-2625

Natural Resources Defense
  Council
40 West 20th Street
New York, NY 10011
(212) 727-2700

Pollution Probe Foundation
12 Madison Avenue
Toronto, Ontario M5R 2S1
Canada
(416) 926-1907

World Resources Institute
1735 New York Avenue NW
Washington, DC 20006
(202) 638-6300

Worldwatch Institute
1776 Massachusetts Avenue NW
Washington, DC 20036
(202) 452-1999

Ambio 18, no. 3 (1989). Issue devoted to air pollution and acid rain.

American Lung Association. *Air Pollution in Your Home.* New York: American Lung Association, 1987.

————. *Health Effects of Air Pollution.* New York: American Lung Association, 1989.

Boyle, Robert H., and R. Alexander Boyle. *Acid Rain.* New York: Schocken Books, 1983.

Brenner, David J. *Radon: Risk and Remedy.* Salt Lake City: Freeman, 1989.

Brown, Michael. *The Toxic Cloud: The Poisoning of America's Air.* New York: HarperCollins, 1988.

Cannon, James S. *Drive for Clean Air: Natural Gas and Methanol Vehicles.* New York: INFORM, 1989.

Eckholm, Eric P. *Down to Earth.* New York: Norton, 1982.

Economic Commission for Europe (ECE). *Air Pollution Across Boundaries.* New York: United Nations, 1985.

Environmental Protection Agency. *Asbestos Fact Book.* Washington, DC: Environmental Protection Agency, 1986.

French, Hilary F. "Clearing the Air: A Global Agenda." In *State of the World 1990: A Worldwatch Institute Report on Progress Toward a Sustainable Society.* Washington, DC: Norton, 1990.

Hunter, Linda Mason. *The Healthy House: An Attic-to-Basement Guide to Toxin-Free Living.* Emmaus, PA: Rodale Press, 1989.

Mackenzie, James J. *Breathing Easier.* Washington, DC: World Resources Institute, 1989.

Mackenzie, James J., and Mohamed El-Ashry, eds. *Ill Winds: Air Pollution's Toll on Trees and Crops.* Holmes, PA: World Resources Institute, 1988.

Miller, G. Tyler, Jr. *Living in the Environment: An Introduction to Environmental Science.* 6th ed. Belmont, CA: Wadsworth, 1990.

Naar, Jon. *Design for a Livable Planet.* New York: HarperCollins, 1990.

National Research Council. *Indoor Air Pollutants.* Washington, DC: National Academy Press, 1981.

Pawlick, Thomas. *A Killing Rain.* San Francisco: Sierra Club Books, 1984.

Postel, Sandra. *Air Pollution, Acid Rain and the Future of Forests.* Washington, DC: Worldwatch Institute, 1984.

Russell, Dick. "L.A.'s Positive Charge." *Amicus Journal* 13, no. 2 (Spring 1991): 18–23. A publication of the Natural Resources Defense Council.

Shute, Nancy. "Driving Beyond the Limit." *Amicus Journal* 13, no. 2 (Spring 1991): 10–17. A publication of the Natural Resources Defense Council.

U.S. Department of Energy. *Clean Coal Technology.* Washington, DC: Department of Energy, 1989.

Weisskopf, Michael. "Lead Astray: The Poisoning of America." *Discover* (December 1988): 68–77.

GLOSSARY

acid deposition   Precipitation or dry deposition containing **sulfuric** and **nitric acids** formed from the burning of **fossil fuels**; commonly known as acid rain.

ambient air quality standards   Limits set on the levels of pollutants allowed in the air. Primary standards are set to protect health; secondary standards protect property and the environment.

asbestos   A material used as insulation in buildings, heating pipes, electrical wiring, and clothing. Crumbling asbestos releases fibers that can become airborne and cause lung disease and cancer if inhaled.

asthma   Respiratory disease in which breathing passages constrict, causing shortness of breath; aggravated by airborne pollutants such as **ozone** and **nitrogen oxide**.

baghouse filter   Vacuum-cleaner-like device consisting of fabric filters that remove particle emissions from exhaust gases in industrial and power plants.

biomass   Organic material—including wood, crops, and dung—that can be burned as fuel; also refers to the total weight of living matter in a given area.

bronchitis   An inflammation of the lung's air passages aggravated by **sulfur dioxide** emissions.

buffering capacity   Ability of soil or bodies of water to naturally neutralize acids.

carbon dioxide   A gas released when fossil fuels are burned. Not normally considered an air pollutant, it is among the **greenhouse gases** that trap heat in the earth's atmosphere, possibly causing a global warming.

carbon monoxide   Odorless, invisible toxic gas that is a product of fossil fuel combustion. Its primary source is motor vehicles.

catalytic converter   Attachment to an automobile that changes pollutants in exhaust gas into less harmful compounds.

chlorofluorocarbons (CFCs)   Gaseous chemicals thought to be the primary cause of the degradation of the earth's protective ozone layer; used as refrigerants, plastic-foam propellants, and in various other industrial processes.

cofiring   Combustion process in which coal and gas are burned at the same time in the same boiler to reduce sulfur and nitrogen oxide emissions.

electrostatic precipitator   A device that electrically charges pollutant particles and then pulls them out of an exhaust stream onto a screen with the opposite electric charge.

emission standards   Pollution control strategy requiring specific sources of pollution—such as power plants—to install control technologies in order to limit emissions.

emphysema   Degenerative lung disease, usually caused by smoking, that is aggravated by ozone pollution.

epidemiological research   Branch of medicine that examines, for example, the health of large numbers of people exposed to everyday pollution levels in a community for long periods of time.

fluidized bed combustion (FBC)   Method that removes sulfur from coal during combustion by mixing crushed coal with limestone and using air jets to suspend the mixture in a boiler. The released sulfur chemically combines with limestone, decreasing the amount of emissions and increasing energy output.

fossil fuels   Combustible materials, including coal, oil, and natural gas, formed over millions of years and under intense pressure and high temperature from the remains of plants and animals.

greenhouse gases   Gases such as **carbon dioxide** and ozone that trap heat in the earth's atmosphere, potentially causing global warming.

gross sustainable productivity   A variation on the gross national product (GNP)—a measurement of the value of goods and services produced by a nation annually—that factors in the depletion of natural resources.

indoor pollution   Pollutants such as tobacco smoke, **asbestos**, formaldehyde, and **radon** that are common in the home and the workplace and can be damaging to health.

lead   A toxic element whose primary atmospheric source is gasoline; can accumulate in the body and eventually damage internal organs.

nitrate   Salt that, with hydrogen, makes up nitric acid; produced in atmospheric reactions involving nitrogen oxides and other compounds.

nitric acid   Acidic compound formed from reactions between nitrogen oxides and water vapor in the atmosphere; a principal constituent of acid rain.

nitrogen oxides   Any of several oxides of nitrogen created when high combustion temperatures cause oxygen and nitrogen to combine chemically; along with sulfur dioxide, is a precursor to acid rain and can react with other substances in the presence of sunlight to form **photochemical smog**.

nuclear energy   Energy source in which heat released by fission, or the splitting of atoms, is converted into electricity.

ozone   Toxic pollutant, consisting of three oxygen atoms (O_3), that is the main component of photochemical smog; formed at ground level by reactions between fossil fuel combustion products and oxygen under the influence of sunlight. Stratospheric ozone, formed higher in the earth's atmosphere, absorbs dangerous ultraviolet radiation, preventing it from reaching the earth and damaging living things.

particulates   Air pollutants in the form of solid particles—such as ash, unburned fuel, and metals—or liquid droplets, such as sulfuric or nitric acid. When inhaled, particulates can travel deep into the lungs and cause serious damage.

photochemical smog   Ozone-containing air pollution created by the action of sunlight upon air pollutants, mostly emitted by motor vehicles.

photovoltaic cells   Solar energy devices that convert sunlight directly into electricity.

pH scale   Measures the acidity or alkalinity of a substance; on the 14-point scale, above 7 (neutral) is alkaline, below 7 is acidic. A substance with a pH of 4 is 10 times as acidic as a substance with a pH of 5.

radon   Naturally occurring radioactive gas released by the decay of radium in the soil. Radon seeps into houses through openings such as cracks in foundations and has been found to cause lung cancer.

reburning   Technique that reduces nitrogen oxide emissions and increases energy efficiency by burning coal with natural gas.

scrubber   Postcombustion device used to remove sulfur from fossil fuel emissions.

solar energy   Energy produced by converting the sun's heat into electricity or other types of usable energy.

sulfate   Salt that, with hydrogen, makes up sulfuric acid; produced in the atmosphere by reactions between sulfur oxides, water, and other compounds.

sulfur dioxide   A pollutant emitted in fossil fuel combustion that, along with nitrogen oxides, is a precursor to acid rain.

sulfuric acid   Acidic chemical formed in the air from reactions between sulfur oxides and water vapor; a principal constituent of acid rain.

thermal inversion   Phenomenon that occurs when a layer of warmer air overlays a layer of colder air, forming an atmospheric lid that traps pollutants close to the earth.

INDEX

PICTURE CREDITS

Conversion Table

(From U.S./English system units to metric system units)

Length

1 inch = 2.54 centimeters
1 foot = 0.305 meters
1 yard = 0.91 meters
1 statute mile = 1.6 kilometers (km.)

Area

1 square yard = 0.84 square meters
1 acre = 0.405 hectares
1 square mile = 2.59 square km.

Liquid Measure

1 fluid ounce = 0.03 liters
1 pint (U.S.) = 0.47 liters
1 quart (U.S.) = 0.95 liters
1 gallon (U.S.) = 3.78 liters

Weight and Mass

1 ounce = 28.35 grams
1 pound = 0.45 kilograms
1 ton = 0.91 metric tons

Temperature

1 degree Fahrenheit = 0.56 degrees Celsius or centigrade, but to convert from actual Fahrenheit scale measurements to Celsius, subtract 32 from the Fahrenheit reading, multiply the result by 5, and then divide by 9. For example, to convert 212° F to Celsius:

$212 - 32 = 180 \times 5 = 900 \div 9 = 100°\ C$

ABOUT THE AUTHOR

EDWARD EDELSON is a former science editor of the *New York Daily News* and a past president of the National Association of Science Writers. His books include *The ABC's of Prescription Narcotics* and the textbook *Chemical Principles* as well as several books for Chelsea House's ENCYCLOPEDIA OF HEALTH series. He has won awards for his writing from such groups as the American Heart Association, the American Cancer Society, the American Academy of Pediatrics, and the American Psychological Society.

ABOUT THE EDITOR

RUSSELL E. TRAIN, currently chairman of the board of directors of the World Wildlife Fund and The Conservation Foundation, has had a long and distinguished career of government service under three presidents. In 1957 President Eisenhower appointed him a judge of the United States Tax Court. He served Lyndon Johnson on the National Water Commission. Under Richard Nixon he became under secretary of the Interior and, in 1970, first chairman of the Council on Environmental Quality. From 1973 to 1977 he served as administrator of the Environmental Protection Agency. Train is also a trustee or director of the African Wildlife Foundation; the Alliance to Save Energy; the American Conservation Association; Citizens for Ocean Law; Clean Sites, Inc.; the Elizabeth Haub Foundation; the King Mahendra Trust for Nature Conservation (Nepal); Resources for the Future; the Rockefeller Brothers Fund; the Scientists' Institute for Public Information; the World Resources Institute; and Union Carbide and Applied Energy Services, Inc. Train is a graduate of Princeton and Columbia Universities, a veteran of World War II, and currently resides in the District of Columbia.